Travels
··········· IN THE ···········
Celtic
World

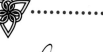

Dear Megan

Happy 16th Birthday!
I hope one day you'll
get to visit this beautiful
place. Maybe until then you
can use the pictures as
your muse until you can
set up your easel on the
Irish moors & let the ghosts
of the Celts inspire you
With Love Always
xo
Morgan

RANNIE GILLIS

TRAVELS
IN THE
CELTIC
WORLD

NIMBUS
PUBLISHING

Nimbus Publishing Limited
P.O. Box 9301, Station A
Halifax, Nova Scotia
B3K 5N5
(902) 455-4286

Design: Neil Meister, GDA, Halifax
Printed and bound in Hong Kong

Canadian Cataloguing in Publication Data
  Gillis, Rannie.

  Travels in the Celtic world

  ISBN 1–55109–092–9 (bound).—
  ISBN 1–55109–129–1 (pbk.)

1. Scotland—Description and travel.
2. Ireland—Description and travel.
3. Cape Breton Island (N.S.)—Civilization—
   Celtic influences. I. Title.

  DA867.5.G45 1994   914.104'85   C94–950105-0

Page viii: *Rural scene, Isle of South Uist, Outer Hebrides.*

This book is dedicated to my mother,

Mary Georgina (MacLean) Gillis,

pianist and music teacher;

and Maria

Acknowledgements

SEVERAL OF THE ESSAYS in this book first appeared in "The Celtic Experience," a column in the *Cape Breton Post* of Sydney, Nova Scotia. Special appreciation is due reporter Wes Stewart, who suggested I write a few articles, and to Managing Editor Fred Jackson, who expanded the assignment into a regular column.

MY SINCERE THANKS to Mary (Jack Malcolm) Gillis, Upper Margaree, and Dougald MacFarlane, Halifax. They shared with me their exceptional knowledge of nineteenth century rural Cape Breton, and provided valuable insight into the state of Celtic culture in the first half of the twentieth century. Fluent in Gaelic, their wit and wisdom represent Celtic 'knowledge' at its finest.

A SPECIAL THANKS to George and Pat MacLean, for assistance and guidance dating back to my years at St. Francis Xavier University, and for a wealth of Celtic information regarding the maternal side of my family.

I WOULD ALSO LIKE TO THANK the following individuals for the important part each played in the preparation of this book:

Catherine Gillis, for reading preliminary drafts of each chapter. Her observations and suggestions were both timely and pertinent, and contributed in no small way to the final result.

Gerry Schuurkamp, for introducing me to the fascinating world of photography, and teaching me the basics of this wonderful art form.

Callista Young, for her skills in proof-reading, and her knowledge of the intricacies of the English language.

Gordon Reid and Ian Lovett, for allowing me to access their knowledge of computers.

Raghu Bhalla, for his valuable insights into the Indo-European origin of the early Celtic peoples. His sincere encouragement provided the original stimulus for this book.

FINALLY, A VERY SPECIAL acknowledgment of my nephew, Christian Gillis, my mother, Mary Gillis, and my sister, Catherine. They spent countless hours, over a four month period, helping me edit approximately 8,000 Celtic transparencies. The nature of their contribution is evident in the selection of photos that accompany the text.

Contents

Preface

I WAS IN THE LEAD, so I noticed it first. However, it is not that easy to bring an eight hundred–pound motorcycle to a stop, so we were well past when I pulled onto the shoulder of the road and Ed Serroul rolled up beside me.

"Did you see those cars, Ed?" I asked.

"Not much room in that parking lot, Rannie."

"Must be a 'ceileidh' of some kind."

"Could be a wedding reception."

"Don't think so. No cars with flowers."

"Let's go back and take a look."

"Whatever it is, we can probably get a cold beer!"

It was shortly after lunch, on an unusually warm Saturday in early October, when I had called Ed and suggested a motorcycle 'run' around the Cabot Trail. It would be a journey of about 250 miles. If we left at one, we could be back home by seven or eight in the evening. Twenty minutes later, Ed's Yamaha 1300 pulled up onto the sidewalk in front of my home.

The two-hour drive from North Sydney to Cape North was a splendid excursion, the kind of trip that makes one happy, and thankful, just to be alive. The tourists were pretty well gone, so the traffic was sparse. It was not quite Thanksgiving weekend, so the 'locals' had not yet begun to take in the fall colours.

We had the narrow, twisting highway pretty much to ourselves. The autumn leaves displayed with every possible colour combination. From scarlet reds to subtle shades of orange, they assaulted the senses at every bend in the road.

When we reached the Englishtown ferry, it was so warm that I peeled off my leather jacket and stowed it in one of the saddlebags. The sunlight reflecting off the waters of St. Anne's Bay was intense, and I took refuge in my polarized sunglasses.

A little over an hour later, we manhandled our motorcycles into a very restricted parking space in front of the Cape North Fire Hall. We were almost exactly half-way around the 'Trail' and, whatever was going on inside, it was time for a break. We might even get lucky and hear some music. We soberly agreed that after half an hour or so—tops—we would hit the road.

As we stepped inside, after paying three dollars apiece at the door, the first thing that caught my eye were the microphones. An array of speakers stood at the ready, on the floor, next to the bar and at the far end of the hall.

"Good news, Ed," I said to my buddy. "Looks like we're going to get some music after all, along with a cold beer. Can't ask for much more than that!"

"Who's playing this afternoon?"

I directed this question to a young man on his way back from the bar. As he delicately tried to balance a small tray crowded with beer, he replied: "Natalie MacMaster and Buddy MacDonald. We're in for a good time."

An understatement if there ever was one!

I turned to Ed and asked if he had ever heard of Natalie McMaster.

"She's the young fiddler from up around the Causeway. I haven't heard her play, but I hear she's pretty damn good."

That turned out to be another understatement!

By the time we were back on the road three hours later, we had experienced an afternoon of Celtic music the likes of which has not been heard by most people outside rural Cape Breton.

Along with the other one hundred or so folks in the hall, we had been entertained by a tall, slim, young woman with a breath-taking, God-given, natural talent.

But Natalie MacMaster is not only one of the fastest rising 'stars' in the new firmament of Celtic music. Nor is she just an attractive blond who happens to play the fiddle.

Along with her musical peers, she is the direct descendant of a long line of Celtic musicians who can trace their ancestry back to a time before the Roman Empire. To a time before Caesar.

Natalie MacMaster.

They came out of the mists of time. The Celts. A strange, unusual, frightening mixture of primitive tribes who were to shape the destiny of Western European civilization and forever change the course of history. For a period of four hundred years, from around 600 to 200 B.C., they were the most powerful people in the western world.

They gave us soap. Women's rights. The rule of law, and Halloween. The distance between the wheels of their war chariots bequeathed to us the gauge of our modern railroad tracks.

The Celts liked to fight. Often. Women as well as men. Some Celts battled naked, totally nude except for a shield and a sword. Others liked to return from a raid with the severed heads of their victims slung from the sides of their horses.

Yet they could break into tears at the sound of music and listen for hours to the stories and poems of their bards. Dancing was considered a gift from the gods and someone who had both musical talent and dancing ability was held in awe.

Such a person, gifted so greatly by the gods, must surely have supernatural affinities. It was as close as you could get to god, and the Celts were deeply religious.

What would the ancient Celts have thought of Natalie MacMaster and her peers, and their raw talent? They take us back to a time when emotion was best expressed through music. Music that was stripped down to its bare essentials: melody and rhythm.

When, hair dishevelled and soaked in sweat, she rose from her chair and started to stepdance while playing a Celtic reel on the fiddle, the emotion in Cape North Fire Hall could no longer be contained.

It was a spontaneous standing ovation, the kind that comes from the soul. The Celtic soul. Men, women, children, senior citizens, and two bikers, all ranted and raved and refused to sit down.

Our Celtic ancestors would have been pleased!

It took one hour to drive from Cape North to Cheticamp, where we gassed up and stopped for supper. When we started out again, the sun was setting and it had turned cold. We stopped to don our heavy sweaters and leather jackets.

Just outside Baddeck, it started to rain. We stopped, removed our leather jackets and put on our rain suits. Then it was up and over Kelly's Mountain, engines throbbing and halogen-beam headlights piercing the rain and the night.

We were each in our own little world—surprisingly warm and cosy, considering the damp, evening chill.

My mind drifted back to some of the places my Yamaha had taken me over the years. Celtic places. The Hebrides. The Scottish Highlands. Ireland. Wales. Brittany in France. Each wondrous, and each in its own special way, unique.

When I pulled up alongside Ed to see how he was getting on, I was startled to hear the Celtic strains of the Barra MacNeils wafting back from the speakers in his windshield.

He gave a little wave, then motioned me to take the lead.
Great music.
A great 'run.'
It was eleven P.M. when we arrived home!

Meat Cove • • Money
Point

THE HIGH CAPES

CAPE BRETON ISLAND
(NOVA SCOTIA, CANADA)

Mabou
Coal • MABOU
Mines HIGHLANDS

• Baddeck*

River Denys
Mountain •
• Highland Village

• Marble Mountain

Little Anse

*Cabot Trail begins and
ends at Baddeck*

Cape Wrath

Isle of Harris
• Applecross

CUILLIN
MOUNTAINS
• Loch Coruisk
Isle of
Rhum Isle of Eigg

SCOTLAND

Isle of Staffa
• Glencoe

Isle of Jura

• Slieve League

• Carrowkeel

• Newgrange

ARAN
ISLANDS IRELAND
Dun Aengus •
THE BURREN

• Glendalough

DINGLE PENINSULA

• Carrantuohill

Skellig Michael •

ENGLAND

the Celtic World
········· Significant Sites ·········
(see pages 114 & 115)

Introduction

WHO WERE THE CELTS and where did they originate?

In order to answer these fundamental questions, we have to go back in time to a period before the formation of the Roman Empire. We will at first be dealing with barbarians, wandering groups of people who had not yet stabilized and reached those advanced stages of social, artistic, and scientific development that would enable us to refer to them as 'civilized.'

There is very little factual knowledge of these barbarians, until we reach the time of the early Greek and Roman historians. To these learned men, a barbarian was simply any person who lived outside the fringes of the Greek or Roman world.

We know that sailors and merchants from ancient Greece and Rome often penetrated and explored the more remote regions beyond the empire and, as a result, came into direct contact with the barbarians. We also know that barbarians often appeared in Greek and Roman cities as slaves and travellers.

Many early Greek and Roman writers were intensely interested in these barbarians who lived on the fringes of the empire. As much as was possible they inquired, with a genuine curiosity, into the manners, morals, and lifestyle of these strange foreigners.

It was the Greeks who called one group of barbarians on their northern borders: 'Keltoi.' They used the term to refer to any of the barbarian tribes who spoke any Celtic language. We do not know, however, whether this name was given them by the Greeks or whether they actually referred to themselves by this name.

('Celts' or 'Kelts'? Either is acceptable. The same is also true for 'Celtic History' or 'Keltic History.')

To the Greeks and Romans, the early Celts presented a striking appearance. Tall, rugged, fair-skinned individuals,

Pre-historic Celts were known to be 'madly fond of war.'

they were very concerned about their appearance. For the most part they wore brightly coloured garments made of linen or wool, which they fashioned themselves. Depending on the season, their footwear would consist of leather sandals or shoes that were usually tied with leather thongs.

Their hair was light in colour, often with a reddish tinge, and they liked to wear it long. They loved to decorate themselves with charms and jewellery, and the women used a wide range of primitive cosmetics.

Aristotle was not too impressed with the Celts he came in contact with, and he referred to them as 'savages.' He wrote: "It is not bravery to withstand fearful things through ignorance. It is not bravery to withstand them through high-spiritedness as when the Celts take up arms to attack the waves."

The Greek historian, Strabo, commented that: "The whole race is madly fond of war, high-spirited and quick

to battle, but otherwise straightforward and not of evil character. They wear ornaments of gold and bracelets on their arms and wrists, while people of high rank wear dyed garments sprinkled with gold. It is this vanity which makes them unbearable in victory and so completely downcast in defeat."

The great Roman historian, Diodorus Siculus, left us a meticulous description of the Celts who lived in modern-day France. "They are tall in stature and their flesh is very white. Their hair is not only naturally blond, but they also use artificial means to increase this natural quality of colour. They continually wash their hair with lime and draw it back from the forehead to the crown and to the nape of the neck. The hair is so thickened by this treatment that it differs in no way from a horse's mane."

He went on to say: "They are exceedingly fond of wine, and drink it greedily. When they become drunk they fall into a stupor or into a crazed disposition. At dinner, a chance remark can move them to anger. An argument can lead to a challenge, which can easily lead to a fight, often to the death. They frequently exaggerate with the aim of praising themselves and diminishing the status of others. They like to boast and threaten and are given to bombastic self-dramatisation. Yet, they are quick of mind and with good natural ability for learning."

It was, however, their ferocious manner and their prowess in battle that spread fear throughout the continent. They were virtually unstoppable in combat. With no apparent fear of death, they took no prisoners and would kill themselves rather than face the ignominy of capture.

To quote Strabo once again: "When the armies are drawn up in battle array they are likely to advance before the battle line and to challenge the bravest of their opponents to single combat. When someone accepts their challenge to battle, they loudly recite the deeds of valour of their ancestors and proclaim their own glorious qualities, at the same time abusing and making little of their opponent."

Many barbaric tribes, in addition to the Celts, have earned their place in the history of western Europe. In relation to the ancient Greco-Roman world, we have the Scythians in the east, the Iberians in the west, and the Germans and Celts in the north and centre. All of these tribes are Indo-European in origin.

The expanding Greek and Roman empires later absorbed all these tribes. Because of their geographical location, the Celts would form an integral part of the Roman Empire and play a most important role in the evolution of modern-day France. They would also play a fundamental role in laying the foundations for modern-day Europe.

When looking back into the origins of the Celts it must be kept in mind that the Celts, as well as the other barbarian tribes, were not a separate race, distinct and different from all others.

The name "Celt" properly refers to a collection of related groups or tribes that inhabited a region of central Europe before the advent of the Greek and Roman Empires. We now know that the earliest of these groups arrived from somewhere farther east, during the early stages of the Bronze Age between 3500 and 2500 B.C.

These tribes spoke a variety of languages, all Celtic in origin. There were very close similarities between these dialects, which were foreign to any other in Europe. But where exactly did the Celts originate?

We know that the Celts were of Indo-European descent. From a linguistic point of view we also know that the Celtic languages were very closely related to the languages of the Indian sub-continent, as well as such other diverse tongues as Iranian and Armenian. This would seem to indicate a common origin somewhere in central Eurasia.

Prehistoric archaeology indicates that sometime around 1500 B.C. the Celts were firmly entrenched in the centre of Europe, where Czechoslovakia is today. Over the next one thousand years, they migrated to western Europe, to the north of the Greek and Roman world.

Although the term "Celt" refers to a collection of related groups or tribes, by 1000 B.C. we can make reference to two major groupings of these tribes on the basis of language: the Brythons and the Goidels.

The fact that these two distinct divisions were based on language implies a fairly clever differentiation between the people who came to speak the two main dialects. It also implies that they were separate for a considerable length of time and that there was a significant interval between the migrations of both groups.

The Brythons, who reached Britain shortly after 1000 B.C., were to spread throughout all of western Europe. By 500 B.C. they were in control of Austria, Switzerland, large portions of France, and most of western Germany. Over the next few hundred years they would expand south into Italy and Spain.

The Goidels reached Ireland in approximately 600 B.C. Almost one thousand years later, shortly after 350 A.D., they spread to the west coast of Scotland. By this time they were known as the Scots.

(The Goidels bequeathed to us Irish and Scotch Gaelic. The Brythons gave us Welsh Gaelic, which is quite different. All three are Celtic in origin.)

How, and why, did the Celts migrate? Well, we must not think of the Celtic expansion as if it were a deliberate and well thought out attempt to conquer and subjugate the known world. It was nothing of the kind.

We must keep in mind that prehistoric populations were partly pastoral and partly agricultural and that they were often quite mobile. They did not always confine themselves to strictly defined borders or frontiers, and they were not comprised of pure racial strains, as such. There was much diffusion and mixing between them.

We must also distinguish mass migrations, which were to come later, from the movements of relatively small numbers of people in the earlier days.

In the beginning, the small groups of Celts who migrated were often led by daring chiefs who were intent on finding new areas for farming and pasturing their animals. Others were simply fearless bands of adventurers or vagabonds, interested in nothing more than pillage and plunder. Many may have migrated simply because of changes in climate, or because of an increase in population density in a certain area.

By the end of the Bronze Age (1000 B.C.), the Celts were numerous and homogeneous enough to travel in relatively large numbers and to set up new settlements, often a considerable distance from "home."

Once the great Celtic migrations started, they continued in successive waves. Each group travelled as far as it could, until it was forced to stop. Often a group would subjugate a previous group of Celts and in so doing, would alter the racial and cultural make-up of its predecessors.

Even though their numbers swelled, there was never a Celtic Empire. The various Celtic tribes were never able to reach the level of co-operation and consolidation that are prerequisites for the development of an empire. They could never see the need for any complex form of political unity and they would certainly never agree to any form of central power, that would confer domination on any one tribe. It was just not in their line of thinking.

The first Celtic colonization of the British Isles (circa 1000 B.C.) was an event of enormous consequence, for it is here that we find the largest of the three surviving Celtic cultures. This culture, which is intact today with living languages and authentic music, comprises three distinct communities.

One such community consists of the Scottish Gaelic speaking inhabitants of the Highlands and Hebrides. Another comprises those people in Wales who speak Welsh Gaelic. Another of these strong Celtic communities is the nation of Ireland.

The largest of the other two surviving Celtic cultures is located just across the English Channel, in that area of north-west France known as Brittany.

To find the third, and by far the smallest, of the surviving Celtic cultures we must cross the Atlantic Ocean and travel two thousand miles to the west. There, on Cape Breton Island, in the province of Nova Scotia, we find a tiny Gaelic speaking community complete with an authentic musical tradition that has recently taken on international proportions.

These few thousand Gaelic-speaking Cape Bretoners form a direct, if very fragile, link with our ancient Celtic ancestors—ancestors who once challenged the might of the Roman Empire and who sent representatives to consider peace talks with Alexander the Great.

By taking a closer look at the early Celtic invasions of the British Isles, we can see that the native inhabitants were assimilated by the invaders, and that this assimilation changed the very nature of the Celts themselves.

That the two strains of Celts, the Brythons in Britain and the Goidels in Ireland and Scotland, remained as distinct entities is attested to by none other than the greatest of the Roman Emperors, Julius Caesar. When he wrote about his first expedition to Britain in 55 B.C., Caesar went out of his way to leave us a first-hand account of the people he found there.

He wrote that the interior of the country was occupied by certain aboriginal tribes, the earliest of whom had arrived in Britain after the end of the last ice age, about 15,000 B.C. He found that the coast areas were occupied by other distinct Celtic-speaking tribes, who were closely relat-

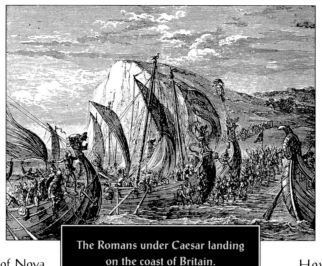

The Romans under Caesar landing on the coast of Britain.

ed to the Celts on the Continent. It was obvious to Caesar that the newcomers had forced the natives from the coast and into the interior.

Although Caesar never reached Ireland, his scouts informed him that the Celtic peoples they found there spoke a language that was quite different from the Celtic languages spoken in Britain.

How and when these Celtic invaders first came to Great Britain, and where they came from, is still a matter of conjecture. We will probably never know for sure, since the answer is lost in the mists of time. Archaeological evidence, based on certain types of swords and axes found in graves, would seem to indicate a date in the vicinity of 1000 B.C.

During the sixth and fifth centuries B.C., a second wave of Celtic invaders reached Britain from the Rhine region of Germany and also from Central Europe.

Another Celtic group arrived around 200 B.C. from the Brittany region of western France, while the last known Celtic invasion took place shortly before the arrival of the Romans. This latter group, a clan known as the Belgae, arrived in Britain after crossing the North Sea from Belgium and Holland.

By the time Caesar and his legions stepped ashore, Celtic had become the dominant language in Britain. The Iron Age culture the Celts had introduced had also spread throughout most of Britain, with the exception of parts of Ireland, the Hebrides, and the northern parts of Scotland.

Caesar found no cities, no large towns, and no trace of any large–scale political organization. The largest social unit was the tribe, under the leadership of a king or chieftain. Even though they were all Celtic, rivalry and open warfare

was rife between the tribes. Some tribes did try to get together with other tribes in order to form stronger units, but most of these attempts were short–lived.

Each tribe was subdivided into a number of smaller units called clans. The members of each clan were closely related to the clan chief and they were all descended from a common ancestor. When a chief died, he was replaced by the oldest competent male member of the clan.

Celtic society was strictly patriarchal and very class conscious, bearing the same type of organization that was found in other primitive societies. At the top were the chief and his nobles. Beneath them were the freemen, who made up the great majority of the clan. At the bottom of clan society were the slaves, who were usually the captured members of the original population.

Like the Romans, the Celts were a very religious people, often worshipping more than one god. Unlike Christians, they did not believe in a 'remote' god, existing in some ill-defined region referred to as heaven. On the contrary, their gods were usually local gods, often associated with nature. A mountain, a river, a lake, a sacred clearing in the forest—all these could be worshipped as deities.

The Celts believed that magic forces controlled every aspect of their daily lives and that these forces could be altered by the use of certain rituals. Sacrifices were an important part of their religious beliefs, usually involving

Druid priests inciting the Britons to resist the Romans.

the use of animals. However, if the occasion was important enough, human sacrifices could be substituted.

Like most prehistoric societies, the Celts had a priestly class. Known as the Druids, they went through a long and vigorous period of training, often lasting fifteen to twenty years. As the Celts had no written language, the Druids were obliged to memorize great quantities of religious text and other pertinent material.

Their main role, in addition to conducting religious ceremonies, was to perform divination. This often involved the use of human sacrifice, a practice which the Romans found particularly offensive. The Druids also preserved the traditions and folklore of the individual tribes, and they fulfilled a need to provide some form of education for the children of the chief and the nobles.

Much of what the Druids did was cloaked in secrecy, which only added to their special standing within the tribe. They were also quick to make use of the magnificent stone circles and burial mounds that had been left by former civilizations of the Middle Stone Age. Places such as Stonehenge in England, Newgrange in Ireland, and the Callanish Standing Stones in the Outer Hebrides were to become closely associated with both the Druids and the practice of Celtic religion.

Because older Druids were often looked upon as magicians and sorcerers, they were often able to exert considerable influence, even over the chief and his warriors. Historians generally believe that it was the Druids who led the Celtic resistance to the introduction of Roman civilization in the British Isles.

Over the next several hundred years, the Celts in the British Isles gradually came under the influence of Roman civilization, except for those in Scotland and Ireland. By 350 A.D., however, Roman rule in Britain was running into difficulty, because Celtic tribes in northeastern Scotland were making daring raids over Hadrian's Wall and into northern England.

At about the same time, another Celtic tribe from Ireland, known as the Scots, started to invade parts of Wales and western Scotland. With in one hundred years, the Scots took up permanent residence in western Scotland and the Hebrides, where they were to give their name to their adopted homeland.

The Romans were also under attack from a different direction. Various Germanic tribes from the Continent started to make hit-and-run raids across the North Sea and into southern England. By 400 A.D., the Romans had begun to withdraw large numbers of soldiers from Britain. They were needed to help with the defence of Italy, which was under increasing attack from various barbarian tribes.

With the defeat of Rome in 476 A.D., the Roman-Celtic inhabitants of the British Isles were left to fend for themselves. Over the next five hundred years, a period usually referred to as "The Dark Ages," tribes of Angles, Saxons, and Jutes, invaded England and permanently settled there. Like the Romans before them, these new invaders left the various Celtic tribes in Ireland, Wales, and Scotland pretty much alone.

The five centuries of Roman rule in Britain had many consequences, the most important of which was the introduction of Christianity. When the first Romans arrived, they did not attempt to convert the various Celtic tribes.

Instead, as in other parts of their Empire, they allowed the native people to continue to worship in their own manner.

The Romans who lived in Britain came from all parts of the far-flung Empire, and they brought with them many gods. One of these religions, from the near east, was Christianity. By the third century A.D., Christians were well established in Roman Britain, flourishing alongside the various Celtic religions.

In the fifth century A.D., St. Patrick brought Christianity to Ireland, where it quickly flourished. In his travels he converted almost the entire population of the small island. In 563 A.D. he sailed to the tiny Hebridean island of Iona and, in the process, introduced Christianity into Scotland. The Celtic religions, based largely on nature worship, were beginning to wane.

With the collapse of the Roman Empire in 476 A.D. came the Dark Ages, and the barbarian hordes spread throughout western Europe and England, destroying civilization and culture. But Celtic Ireland remained untouched by the barbarian invasions. Helped along and encouraged by the Christian Church, culture and learning, as well as the other aspects of civilization, continued to flourish on this little island.

During the Dark Ages, Celtic Ireland became known as the "home of saints and scholars." Individuals came from all parts of Britain and the continent to live and study there. The Irish monasteries, which came to be centres of learning and culture, reached a Golden Age. For a period of five hundred years, Ireland carried the torch of knowledge. As such, it was primarily responsible for preserving culture and civilization in the British Isles.

As the Dark Ages came to a close in the eighth and ninth centuries, Irish missionaries and scholars spread Christianity throughout England, Scotland, and western Europe. In addition to spreading the Christian faith, they reintroduced scholarship and learning, founding schools and monasteries wherever they went.

By the time of the Norman conquest of England in 1066 A.D., the Anglo-Saxons controlled all of Britain, except for large parts of Wales and most of Scotland. Ireland, having never been occupied by the Romans or the Anglo-Saxons, was entirely Celtic.

During the later Middle Ages (1200-1500 A.D.), even though the Norman kings of England consolidated their political control over Ireland, Scotland, and Wales, the Celtic regions of these areas were pretty much left to their own devices. While great political struggle and turmoil went on all about them, these Celtic societies continued on, for the most part, according to custom.

It is now time to focus this brief history on the two Celtic groups with which I am most familiar; the Celts of Ireland and the Celts of Scotland from approximately 1200 A.D. to the present day.

Since the late Middle Ages, various English kings have tried to stamp out the Celtic heritage in Wales and Scotland. By and large, their efforts failed, except in the lowland region of Scotland. The Highlands and Hebrides, as well as most of Wales, remained solidly Celtic.

During this period there were many rebellions against British rule in Scotland, none of them very successful. The most famous of these uprisings took place in August, 1745, when a young 'Pretender to the Scottish Throne' set sail from exile in France and landed in the western Highlands of Scotland.

During the 'Dark Ages,' Irish monasteries became centres of learning and culture.

When Prince Charles Edward Stuart (Bonnie Prince Charlie) stepped ashore in August of that year, he fully expected that all of the Scottish clans would come together and join with his meagre forces to drive the British from Scotland.

Most of the Celtic clans, from the Highlands and the Hebrides, did unite behind the young prince. The lowland clans, having being more exposed to British culture and society, did not. Nevertheless, the ragged clan army of the young prince surprised just about everyone and captured the cities of Perth and Edinburgh.

Next, they advanced into northern England. However, a lack of supplies and reinforcements soon forced them to retreat back into Scotland. The British regrouped and, led by the Duke of Cumberland, pursued the weary Highland army. The British forces were joined by clans from the lowlands as they followed the prince's army north. On 16 April, 1746, the two armies met on a barren highland moor, not far from the town of Inverness.

Prince Charlie had approximately five thousand Highlanders and Hebrideans in his force. Most had been fighting, then retreating, for the past ten months. They were cold, hungry, dead-tired, and very disappointed that their lowland 'Celtic cousins' did not join their cause. Physically worn out, they had reached the limit of their endurance.

The Duke of Cumberland had approximately nine thousand men, the vast majority of whom were well fed, well rested, and well supplied.

The Battle of Culloden Moor was anything but 'a battle.' It was a rout. A slaughter. A disaster. The Highland ranks broke. Those who did not die on the battlefield were pursued into the surrounding hills and killed, without mercy. The Duke did not take prisoners.

For days afterwards, the Duke's soldiers sought out survivors of the battle and killed them in cold blood. Any inhabitants of the region who gave help to wounded or fleeing Highlanders were also killed—women and children too.

Today, in the Highlands, the Duke of Cumberland is referred to as 'Butcher Cumberland'!

With the defeat of Bonnie Prince Charlie's Highland Army, the British government decided once and for all to put an end to any possible future insurrections in the Highlands and the Hebrides.

This involved the elimination of the clan system. In the fall of 1746 the British Parliament passed the Disarming Act, which prohibited any clansman from bearing arms or weapons. Another Act prohibited the wearing of the kilt, or clan tartan. Bagpipes, which were often used with great effect to lead the clans into battle, were also prohibited.

In actual fact, the Battle of Culloden Moor marked the beginning of a period of rapid decline in the Celtic culture of Scotland. Within a period of fifty years, the infamous Highland Clearances were under way and the mass migration, and dispersion, of the Celtic Scot had begun.

It is estimated that in the 150 years following the Battle of Culloden Moor, more than 250,000 Celtic emigrants left the Highlands and the Hebrides. A substantial number of these came to British North America and settled in the Maritime provinces.

However, it must be kept in mind that a small number of Scots had come to Canada in the years before the defeat at Culloden Moor. As far back as 1621, Sir William Alexander had been granted a charter by the Crown to establish a colony in Nova Scotia. He set up small settlements on the mainland and on Cape Breton Island and he christened the new colony with the Latin name for 'New Scotland.'

The Scottish settlers, however, were poorly prepared for the rigours of a Canadian winter and the settlements did not survive. In 1632, all Scottish claims to the region were surrendered to France.

Between 1745 and 1820 almost twenty thousand Scottish immigrants came to the Maritimes. Ninety percent of these were Gaelic speaking Roman Catholics from the Highlands and the Hebrides. In the early part of the nineteenth century, Gaelic was actually the third most common European language spoken in Canada, after English and French!

Between 1820 and 1870, a further 175,000 Scottish immigrants crossed the Atlantic, including a sizeable number of Protestants from the lowland regions of the old country.

After 1850, most of the Scottish people who came to Canada bypassed the Maritimes and Quebec and settled in Ontario and western Canada. This trend has continued to the present day.

Although the Scots, like most ethnic groups, were eventually assimilated into the mainstream of Canadian society, they nevertheless retained an awareness of their unique heritage. In most cases this awareness has been closely tied to the very symbols that were prohibited after the rebellion in 1745, the kilt, the tartan, the bagpipe, and the various clan societies.

It is either in spite of this process of assimilation, or because of it, that a small enclave of Celtic culture on Cape Breton Island has retained its authentic roots to the present day.

The Gaelic language is surviving, in Cape Breton, albeit barely. At best there are a few thousand people, most of them elderly, who are fluently conversant in the ancient tongue. Isolated attempts that have recently been made to reintroduce Gaelic into elementary schools in Inverness and Victoria counties have not met with much success.

Celtic music, on the other hand, has undergone a tremendous resurgence, something that would have been considered unthinkable only a generation ago. In the early 1970s, three young Irish immigrants in St. John's, Newfoundland, formed the folk group Ryan's Fancy. All excellent musicians, they became very popular, but only in a narrow, regional sense. Like many others, they were ahead of their time.

Recently, authentic Celtic groups like the Rankin Family from Mabou, and the Barra MacNeils from Sydney Mines, have gained not only national, but international, status. Talented soloists like Howie MacDonald, John Morris Rankin, Ashley MacIssac, and Natalie MacMaster, have rekindled an interest, especially among the young, in the authentic music of their forefathers.

And then there is Rita MacNeil, truly an international Celtic superstar. In her own words and music she carries on the Celtic tradition of the ancient 'bard,' passing on knowledge and folklore in a highly entertaining manner.

In addition to the Scottish immigrants who came to the Maritime provinces and established Gaelic communities, the Irish settlers crossed the Atlantic to escape English hegemony.

The story of the Irish migration began around 1200 A.D., when English, Welsh, and Norman colonists appeared in various parts of Ireland in an attempt to subjugate the country. The Pope began to exercise greater control over the Irish Church, which up until then had pretty well gone its own way.

At the end of the Middle Ages, the British did have some success in planting colonies in southeastern Ireland. However, by the end of the fifteenth century, these areas had shrunk to a small region around the city of Dublin.

To protect the lives and property of English settlers and merchants, a fortified earthen rampart known as 'The Pale' was constructed, at great expense, around this English community.

Anyone living outside this fortified area was considered to be 'Beyond the Pale.' This, by definition, included the entire Celtic population of Ireland.

By the sixteenth century, there was a great deal of conflict between the native Celtic population and the English administration. The situation was not helped when the English attempted to impose the beliefs of the Protestant Reformation on the Irish Catholics.

The next two hundred years were marked by a large influx of English, Welsh, and Scottish settlers. This was accompanied by a long, violent period of rebellion and conquest. By the beginning of the eighteenth century, England had assumed complete control in Ireland.

The old Celtic order was gone. Every attempt was made to eradicate any trace of Celtic culture and language. Protestant administrators acted, for the most part, as if Irish Catholic society did not exist. The native population was suppressed socially, politically, and economically.

It was around this time that the Irish began to emigrate in large numbers, and many of them came to Atlantic Canada.

The Irish connection with Canada goes back at least fourteen hundred years, if you believe the ancient Irish journals which state that St. Brendon the Bold, the Irish missionary and navigator, reached the shores of the new world sometime during the sixth century A.D.!

Be that as it may, we do know that since the seventeenth century there have been Irish in Atlantic Canada, mainly due to military ties between France and the south of Ireland. Irish fishermen have also lived in Newfoundland since the early eighteenth century and we can safely surmise that they came here to fish long before that.

In the early nineteenth century, an expanding economy in British North America, combined with a steadily deteriorating economy at home, convinced many destitute Irish that the time was right to pull up stakes. Since these immigrants were usually quite poor, most could not afford to move on to central or western Canada and therefore remained in the Maritime provinces.

Unlike the Scottish settlers who tended to seek out agricultural land and set up farming communities, the Irish gravitated towards port cities such as St. John's and Halifax. When they moved to rural areas, the Irish tended to seek out employment as opposed to farming.

The Irish Potato Famine of 1845-1848 led to the death of many thousands and forced almost two million people to emigrate. Of these, hundreds of thousands came to Atlantic Canada where, like the Irish before them, they settled in towns and cities. By 1870 the Irish comprised the largest ethnic group in every large city and town in the Atlantic region!

The desire for Irish independence gained momentum by the beginning of the twentieth century with the growth of a strong Nationalist movement. The Easter Rising in 1916 was the first of several armed incidents that indicated the end of British rule in Ireland was close at hand.

When independence came in 1921 Ireland became a dominion within the Empire. Twenty-six of Ireland's thirty-two counties joined the new nation. The other six, all with a large Protestant majority, remained part of Great Britain. We are all aware of what has happened since, in Northern Ireland!

As we have seen, events in Scotland and in Ireland in the eighteenth and nineteenth centuries forced the greatest Celtic migrations in nearly 2,000 years to occur worldwide.

We can best appreciate the extent of the Celtic migrations to Atlantic Canada during the last two centuries by referring to the Federal Census of 1961. This was the last census to identify Canadians on the basis of their ethnic background.

Final tallies indicated that people of Scottish and Irish descent made up the third and fourth largest ethnic groups in Canada, after the French and the English. Rounded off, the statistics for the Atlantic provinces were as follows:

	English	Scottish	Irish
Nova Scotia	211,000	183,000	94,000
New Brunswick	158,000	81,000	82,000
Prince Edward Island	30,000	33,000	20,000
Newfoundland	342,000	10,000	75,000

According to these statistics, in 1961, people of Celtic descent (493,000) made up the greatest proportion of the population (892,000) in the three Maritime provinces (Nova Scotia, New Brunswick, and Prince Edward Island).

When we include Newfoundland, we find that Atlantic Canada at that time had 578,000 people of Celtic descent out of a total population of 1,319,000!

The Grand Tour

THE SOUND WAS UNIQUE. Soft and mellow. Not at all like the sound of a modern concert grand piano, of the kind that Steinway and Baldwin make. No, this was something different, and it fascinated me.

I had never before played a Silbermann, nor had I even heard of one. I was politely informed that the instrument had been built in Germany, about 1730, by the gentleman whose name it bore and that his instruments had been the rage in European musical circles at that time.

Johann Sebastian Bach played, and composed, on one. King Frederick the Great of Prussia, a highly respected amateur musician, was so impressed by the instrument that he collected fifteen of them.

When I expressed an interest in trying the instrument, the tour guide in Brodick Castle was reluctant. I prevailed, assuring her that I could, indeed, play the piano, and the vocal encouragement of several onlookers swayed her to allow me to try.

Since the great Bach himself had been an enthusiastic admirer of this brand of piano, what better piece to start with than the opening number of that great body of piano studies that he composed, known as 'The Well Tempered Clavier.'

Carefully placing my leather motorcycle jacket on the side of a sofa, I sat down at the keyboard and, with some degree of trepidation, started to play. The opening notes of the Prelude and Fugue Number One in C Major seemed to merge perfectly with the lavish decor of this drawing room. This music—simple, yet elegant—was an eloquent reflection of the type of society for which it had been intended. The same could be said for this room in Brodick Castle.

Although the oldest part of the castle was built in the twelfth century, this drawing room was a much later addition, dating from the seventeenth century.

I followed the Bach selection with the opening movement of Beethoven's Moonlight Sonata. By this time the size of my audience had grown from the original four to about five times that number, and the volume of applause had increased appropriately.

Sensing that the group wanted another selection and, throwing caution to the wind, I immediately launched into a form of jazz known as 'Boogie-Woogie.' As my left hand laid down a steady walking beat in the bass, my right hand began to play those simple variations on a basic blues theme that make this form of jazz so infectious, and entertaining, to listen to.

As I gradually increased the tempo, I changed my left hand pattern from a simple walking bass to a rhythmically more advanced 'honky-tonk' pattern. This is the sort of tune that would bring a round of applause, when I used to play at variety concerts while attending St. Francis Xavier University in Antigonish.

It had the same effect here. These were individuals who were obviously familiar with Bach and Beethoven, yet they could not resist the rhythmic impulse and irresistible good humour of jazz. I was obliged to play two more jazz numbers before I was allowed to rise from the keyboard.

I was later told that if I ever returned to the Isle of Arran I would have unlimited access to Brodick Castle, this drawing room, and this piano. The guide pointed out that I was probably the first pianist to ever play Boogie-Woogie on a Silbermann grand piano!

This is just one example of the kind of reception that I, a Celtic Canadian, experienced during my first visit to Scotland. I had just spent two weeks touring in England and Wales. The Isle of Arran was the first Hebridean island I came upon.

Irish Gaelic and English road signs,
County Galway, Republic of Ireland.

I was travelling without benefit of an itinerary. Instead, I had decided to give myself free rein to follow a map and pick out the places that interested me. When I came across places such as the Isle of Arran, I was usually reluctant to leave.

After crossing to Arran on the late afternoon ferry I had proceeded very slowly along the main street looking for a bed and breakfast facility.

"I watched you arrive in the village this afternoon. It reminded me of a scene from one of your American cowboy movies. A stranger comes into town. No one has seen him before. The size of that motorcycle just made people stop and stare."

I had not planned it that way, I told the postmaster in a local pub.

The motorcycle was no more than a means of transportation, a way of experiencing the countryside in a manner that could only be equalled by walking (which would have been too slow), or perhaps by a pedal bike (which would have been too slow and strenuous). As it turned out, the bike provided a wonderful way to meet people, once the initial shock wore off.

Built for the North American touring market, and weighing in at eight hundred pounds, it was considered a massive machine in the British Isles. Its engine (1100 cc) was larger than the engines found in most cars.

Keeping a respectful distance, most people would just stop and stare. Young people, however, would gather round the bike and examine it from every angle, while the more daring of the boys would ask to sit on it. Older people, especially in the Highlands and the Hebrides, were very often intimidated, and not only by the machine.

I often went for days without shaving and this, along with the leather jacket, the helmet, and dark sunglasses, conspired to keep them away. Those who recognized the Canadian flag that was prominently displayed on the bike would usually relax. Once they found out that I was just a high school guidance counsellor/photography instructor on summer vacation, there was no end to their hospitality.

I must say that I felt quite at home during this first visit to Scotland, in the summer of 1980, and it was not as if I had come unprepared. During my years at St. Francis Xavier University in Antigonish I had studied Celtic history, Celtic literature, and Gaelic.

I vividly remember being recalled to St. F.X. from the deck of the S.S. Burgeo, on dry dock in St. John's, Newfoundland. I had not planned to attend my graduation ceremonies because it was my intention to return to university in order to get another degree, in Education. Besides, I needed the money from my summer job as a steward in the Newfoundland Coastal Service.

It seems I was to receive an award, and not just any award. The Angus L. MacDonald Award for Celtic Studies, named after a former premier of Nova Scotia, was considered by some to be one of the more prestigious awards given by the university. Furthermore, I was to receive two hundred dollars in cash.

The Department of Celtic Studies had only one instructor, but what a fascinating man he was. Calum Ian

Yamaha 1100. Touring motorcycle, 'North American Style.' Such big bikes are built for only two world markets: North America and Australia.

(Malcolm John) MacLeod was perhaps the most gifted Gaelic poet of his generation.

Born in Scotland in 1913, Calum distinguished himself in the field of Celtic Studies while a student at the University of Edinburgh, where he won several Gold Medals. At the age of twenty-four, he received national recognition at the Gaelic Mod (Festival) in Dundee with the award of the title 'Bard.' He was the youngest person ever to receive such an honour. An accomplished master of the bagpipe, he was often called upon to play at important campus functions, especially those of a political nature.

As impressive as his academic credentials were, his students were more taken with the fact that he had served with the British Army in the North African desert during World War Two. Known around campus as 'Major MacLeod,' he was a powerfully built man who always wore his kilt and full Scottish dress, even on the coldest day in winter. This was just one of many traits that endeared him to his students.

While his classes in Celtic Literature and Celtic History were usually filled, there were only three students in his Gaelic classes, and they were all from Cape Breton. Looking back now, it is evident that while Celtic Literature and History students came from all parts of the Maritimes, only students from Cape Breton held an interest in the ancient Celtic language.

This comes as no surprise because it is only on Cape Breton Island that you can find individuals who still speak the language fluently. And that was certainly true in the case of my family.

Sheep farm on the Isle of Mull, Inner Hebrides.

My father was fluent in Gaelic, as were his seventeen brothers and sisters. Having been raised on a farm in Upper Margaree, they were still part of the active and vigorous Celtic culture of Inverness County.

My mother, on the other hand, who had been born and raised in North Sydney, was not. Even though her parents and all her aunts and uncles were fluent in Gaelic, hers was an urban generation that had lost the Celtic language, keeping only the Celtic musical tradition.

The other two students in my Gaelic class were cut from the same cloth. Angus Beaton, from Mabou, came from a long line of Gaelic speakers as did Linden MacIntyre from Port Hastings.

Angus, who teaches school in Mabou, still speaks to me in Gaelic whenever we meet. Linden, who is now a respected (and award–winning) correspondent with one of our national television networks, has less of an opportunity to practice the old language. Except, of course, when he returns to Cape Breton.

During my early, impressionable years, I was exposed to the very finest in Celtic traditional music and dancing during the many 'ceilidhs' that were held in my home. Winston Fitzgerald, Angus Chisholm, Joe MacLean, Bill Lamey, Johnny Wilmot; these and many other musicians, singers, and dancers were frequent visitors.

My father, Ambrose, played the violin, as did several uncles, while my mother, Mary, is well known as a Celtic piano player. My grandfather, Malcolm Gillis, was known as the Margaree Bard in recognition of his many Gaelic songs and poems. I was surprised to discover that

The Scottish Highlands. On the mainland across from the Isle of Skye.

many of his songs are well known in Scotland, especially in the Hebrides!

Thus, even from a very early age, I was exposed to all manner of things Scottish, or as we would say today, Celtic. Like many other Nova Scotians of Scottish descent who came of age in the sixties, I wanted to make a trip to 'The Old Country,' a visit that had been out of the realm of possibility for most of our parents and grandparents.

The idea of renting a car with several other people, or taking a bus tour, did not appeal to me. I also knew from the experience of others, including my sister, that hitch-hiking was not the way to travel. One or more individuals, with large knapsacks, would find it very difficult to physically fit into the small cars that are common in Scotland, Ireland, and other parts of the British Isles.

In the summer of 1978, I took a six-week, six thousand mile motorcycle tour from Nova Scotia to New Orleans on the Gulf of Mexico. It was this trip that convinced me to tour Scotland and the rest of the British Isles by motorcycle.

Without the steel box that surrounds you when travelling by car, you travel with the environment, rather than through it. You are very much aware of the sights, the sounds, and even the smells that accompany your voyage and, somewhat like those who follow the sea, you always keep one eye on the weather.

The stage was set and in the winter of 1979 and 1980, the decision was made. I would ship the motorcycle by boat from Halifax to London and fly over as soon as school let out. I planned to pick up the bike in London and set out for a nine–week tour of the ancient Celtic world.

Realizing that the original homeland of the Celtic peoples was off-limits, because it was behind the Iron Curtain, I was still determined to visit those parts of Western Europe and the British Isles that had at one time been within the Celtic realm.

In those nine weeks, I would cover 7,500 miles and visit eleven countries, most of which had played a part in the Celtic saga. Four of those weeks (and three thousand miles) were spent in Scotland. England, Wales, and Ireland each received one week, while I had to make do with spending only two weeks in Celtic Europe.

I must admit that in spite of my Celtic background, my Celtic studies at university, and all my advanced preparation and planning, I was totally unprepared for what I encountered in Scotland.

I was swept away by the sheer magnitude of it all; the stark and barren highlands, the lonely lochs, and the mist–shrouded islands of the Hebrides. Most haunting of all, however, were the empty glens, or valleys. For it was from places such as these that our ancestors had been evicted and forced, without compassion, to emigrate to Canada, the United States, Australia, and New Zealand.

Before I reluctantly left for Ireland, I had already made up my mind to return. With only one week to devote to 'The Emerald Isle,' I failed to realize that it would have the same effect.

Over the next thirteen years I would return to both Scotland and Ireland many times. I biked, walked, hiked, and talked. At least twice a week, I recorded my impressions and observations in a small log book. I took lots of colour slides so that I could share my travel experiences with others. Thanks

My first view of the Hebrides. The Isle of Arran, Inner Hebrides, on the Horizon.

to these logs, and a collection of colour slides that now number close to eight thousand, I can relive these Celtic journeys whenever I wish.

What follows, then, is an exploration of our unique Celtic legacy, with particular emphasis on Scotland and Ireland. It is my hope that these essays, which do not follow a strict chronological order, ignite an interest in further delving into our Celtic world. Your own journey could begin at the local library, and if it's a university library, the selection of Celtic titles will be much greater.

Should you choose to begin your exploration of the Celtic world with a visit to either Scotland or Ireland, be prepared for a strong urge to return, again and again.

Finally, the Celtic experience is, in fact, close at hand. I refer, of course, to the rural areas of Cape Breton Island, where you can still find pockets of the ancient language and visit the places that spawned the current revival of Celtic music.

We should also be aware that the French-speaking areas of Cape Breton and mainland Nova Scotia have many direct ties to the ancient Celtic world. Many of the early settlers in these regions were from the Brittany region of France. As such, they are our Celtic 'cousins,' and their language, customs, and music offer further riches for the culturally curious.

This, then, is a highly personal view of the Celtic world, past and present. It is not a perfect place, as the ongoing events in Northern Ireland continue to prove, but then the Celtic world never was. It is, however, a special place. A place to get in touch with your past. A place to get it touch with your soul.

Megaliths

"HELLO. I WONDER if I could get some directions?"

The elderly couple had not noticed my approach, as they were engrossed in the act of erecting their tent.

"Are you lost?"

"No. Not really. But I can't seem to find the Standing Stones that are indicated on the Ordnance Survey map."

"Well I don't think you will have any luck at all in locating those Standing Stones."

"Why's that?"

"Well, the Standing Stones you are seeking are no longer standing."

"What do you mean?"

"They are no longer in a vertical position. They are now in a horizontal position, as in, flat on the ground."

"What happened to them?"

"They fell down, or heaven knows, they might even have been pushed."

"Why would someone do that?"

"Can't say, old boy. I'm only a visitor here myself. Are you American?"

"No. Canadian."

"Jolly good. We're British. From Oxford. You've heard of it?"

"Yes, its a university town. You have a boat race every year with Cambridge."

"Bang on, old chap! We always give the blighters a run for their money. Tell me, Canada, if a Standing Stone is no longer standing, is it still a Standing Stone?"

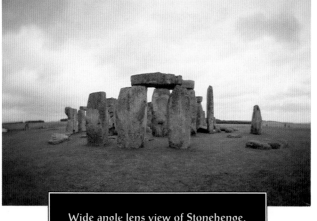

Wide angle lens view of Stonehenge. This type of lens serves to highlight the very unusual nature of such a prehistoric monument.

"Leave it to someone from Oxford to come up with a philosophical question like that."

"Yes, well, I must think about that. Anyway, Canada, if you continue southwest for about another quarter mile, in that direction there, you'll find your 'reclining' Standing Stones. Off you go!"

I had stumbled across this pair, quite by accident, in a little gully on the west coast of the Isle of Barra, in the Outer Hebrides. They were obviously determined to get away from it all, and they had picked the right spot to do so.

As for myself, the sun had begun to set in the west, so I decided to put off my visit to the Non-standing Stones.

It was really not all that important. There are an estimated sixty thousand stone monuments in western Europe, and in a few days time I would be able to revisit the site of the second largest such complex in the British Isles.

These mysterious monuments are generally made up of either individual stones or complex arrangements of massive boulders. The greatest of them involves the accumulation of large mounds of earth and rock, often hundreds of feet in diameter. Often referred to as 'megaliths' (Greek: megas=big; lithos=stone), they are usually divided into three groups:

Single standing stones, known as 'menhirs' in Brittany. The largest such stone ever erected by man is located near

Callanish Standing Stones.

Carnac in France. It was sixty-six feet high and weighed over three hundred tons. Today, it lies on the ground, broken in four pieces.

Stone Circles, such as Stonehenge in England and Callanish in the Outer Hebrides, are standing stones placed so as to form a circle. Rows of standing stones are often associated with these circles.

Graves with large stone roofs. Also known as dolmens, passage graves, and chambered tombs.

When I first visited the Callanish Standing Stones on the Isle of Lewis in the Outer Hebrides, I had to share the sacred site with two bus loads of Dutch and German tourists. I examined the area as best I could, took some pictures, and was back on my motorcycle in less than thirty minutes. That was in August, 1980.

When I returned to the site in August, 1993, I was alone. It was also late in the evening, after I had spent the better part of the day exploring less imposing sites in the vicinity. I remained until well after dark.

In the intervening years I had read just about everything I could get my hands on regarding the origin and development of these prehistoric stone monuments. Yet, I was still staggered by the sheer magnitude of these obelisks, these temples in stone.

Although they preceded the Celtic era in Britain and Ireland by two thousand years, the stone monuments in these areas were often tied in with Celtic religious beliefs and customs. If they did not construct them, the Celts were among the first to adapt them to their own needs.

Consider the Celtic priesthood known as the Druids. Almost anyone you ask will tell you that the Druids built Stonehenge, on the rolling pastures of southern England. That they used the site as a religious temple, and their rituals often involved the use of human sacrifice. When pressed further, they will probably state that the site was also used for astronomical forecasting.

The Druids, of course, did not build Stonehenge. In fact, construction began about 2700 B.C.—over 1,500 years before the Celts reached Britain—and it continued on and off for well over one thousand years.

Stonehenge consists of several ditches and earthen ramparts, as well as several concentric stone circles. Its outer perimeter ditch is 380 feet in diameter, while some of its larger 50-ton blocks of stone came from Wales, a distance of over 100 miles!

The question of whether Stonehenge and other stone circles were built for astronomical purposes, or for purely religious reasons, remains unanswered. But, the question of whether the Celts used such sites for religious rituals can be answered with a resounding 'yes.'

However, there is no valid archaeological evidence to suggest that these sites were ever used for human sacrifice. There is also no evidence to support the theory that they have been used as places to live. They seem to have been constructed solely for religious reasons.

For astro-archaeologists, the Callanish circle ranks second only to Stonehenge. However, compared to Stonehenge which is only an hour's drive from London, the remote location of the Callanish group assures that it receives only a fraction of the visitors, and a corresponding fraction of the publicity.

Its nucleus consists of a chambered cairn (stone graves with many chambers) within a stone circle, with four rows of standing stones leading off in different directions. It was built in the third millennium B.C. and is thus approximately the same age as Stonehenge.

Those of us who remember our history lessons from school, especially those chapters pertaining to the origin of civilization, can summon a vague recollection of the Fertile Crescent. This fertile, crescent-shaped strip of land on the eastern shore of the Mediterranean has often been referred to as 'The Cradle of Civilization.'

Stonehenge. The horizontal capstone on the right of this photo weighs in excess of fifty tons. How was it transported from a quarry in Wales, over one hundred miles away, and how was it put in place on top of the vertical pillars?

Stretching from the shores of the Persian Gulf, up through the valleys of the Tigris and Euphrates Rivers, and curving westwards towards Egypt and the valley of the Nile, it was the home of the earliest civilizations in Europe and the Middle East.

Assyria; Babylon; Ancient Egypt; these and other less famous regimes left their mark on the development of civilization.

Yet, at the same time, thousands of miles to the west, the imagination and ingenuity of peoples in western Europe produced a staggering collection of structures that rival, if not in some ways exceed, the vastly more famous structures such as the pyramids of Egypt and the Hanging Gardens of Babylon.

The Neolithic (Late Stone Age) people who built these incredible monuments were a mixture of primitive farmers and hunter-gatherers who came from the eastern parts of Europe, beginning sometime around 6000 B.C.

They could not write, so they left behind no written records. They developed neither cities nor city-states and never formed nations. Yet, as the evidence in stone so readily demonstrates, they were capable of organization on a truly grand scale and of designing and erecting hugely complex and daunting engineering 'mega-projects.'

These megaliths stretch from the island of Malta in the Mediterranean, through Spain and Portugal, into France and the British Isles, and as far north as Denmark.

What is most awesome about these structures, aside from their size and complexity, is the fact that the primitive Stone Age farmers and hunter-gatherers who built them were the first people in history to make a conscious and

Eroded limestone plateau in front of Passage Grave in the Bricklieve Mountains, Irish Republic. It is possible to make out a circular stone 'foundation,' which is all that remains of one of the dwellings used by the people who made the graves.

well-thought out effort to erect stone structures and monuments that were designed to last forever.

They were built over a period of approximately three thousand years, beginning sometime around 4000 B.C., and the earliest of them predate the earliest Egyptian pyramids!

While there is intense speculation as to the true purpose of the standing stones and stone circles, the true nature of the dolmens, passage graves, and chambered tombs is undisputed. They were used as burial sites, and the archaeological evidence is there to prove it.

One such site, the Carrowkeel Passage Graves, is located in the remote Bricklieve mountains, in County Sligo, in western Ireland. The day I ventured into these mountains, all alone in spite of the protestations of my boarding lady, I had to hike several miles from where I left my motorcycle.

The hike and the solitude were not a problem. My main concern was whether or not it was going to rain, and if there would be any mist. Rather than face that sort of weather, I would have far preferred to spend the rest of the day in a nice, cosy pub.

I encountered showers, but they were light, and the mist never appeared. Mist (low-lying cloud) and mountains do not go together at all, as it is too easy to become disoriented and lose your way.

The invigorating walk required that I traverse across the base of one mountain and make a steep climb up the back of another. The route took me across a flat, open area of eroded limestone. There, I was able to make out the ruins of the stone huts that had housed the prehistoric workers who built the tombs on the mountain tops.

Entrance to Passage Grave on first summit, Irish Republic.

Once on top, I found myself on a small plateau, with three mounds of stones indicating the location of the three passage graves. On the summits of several other mountains I could easily make out the locations of eleven more passage graves. (A passage grave has a narrow tunnel leading to an inner burial chamber. The entire unit was covered by a mound of stone and rock.)

It was as if I were all alone in the world. The view was overwhelming; a stunning panorama broken only by the nearby peaks with their mounds of stone.

I had been told that entering one of the passage graves would be quite safe. After all, it had not collapsed in over four thousand years!

After removing my backpack, I took my flashlight and camera, and squeezed into the narrow opening. But I could not venture far on my hands and knees, and was forced to back out. I had not come this far to be held back by a narrow passage!

So I lay down on my back and slowly inched my way through the miniature passage. After a distance of about twenty feet, I was able to stand up, with room to spare. I was looking at the inside of my first passage grave.

I knew that the interior had been excavated in the early years of this century, and that human bones had been found, along with shards of broken pottery and other artifacts. The bones were then carefully reburied, while the artifacts were brought to Dublin University.

The floor, walls, and roof of the entrance passage were made of large, flat pieces of rock. The roof of the interior chamber was comprised of immense, flat pieces of stone that were up to six inches thick and eight feet long. They overlapped each other in such a manner that there was a

Tallest Standing Stone in Scotland (nineteen feet),
Isle of Lewis, Outer Hebrides.

good five feet of space over my head, in the centre of the chamber, and perhaps one foot or more, off to the sides.

Most intriguing of all were the three little chambers that surrounded the central one. Radiating from the centre like spokes on a wheel, they probably contained the personal belongings of my pre-Celtic ancestors who had been interred there.

Detailed studies had also indicated that the setting sun lights up this inner chamber on the longest day of the year (the summer solstice). This neat little trick, requiring an intimate knowledge of astronomy, was reminiscent of some of the Egyptian tombs and temples that had been found along the banks of the Nile. My pre-Celtic cousins, however, managed to perfect this bit of wizardry almost a thousand years earlier!

While I was inside, a heavy rain pounded on the mound for about twenty minutes. Had I been outside, I would have been drenched. Instead, I was nice and cosy; not a drop of water entered the inner chamber—a tribute to the construction skills of those who had built this grave more than four thousand years ago.

Two days later I was admiring my second passage grave at Newgrange, on the banks of the River Boyle, about thirty miles from Dublin. Built sometime in the fourth millennium B.C., it is an extraordinary feat of architecture and engineering and is rightly considered to be one of the most spectacular prehistoric monuments in western Europe.

An estimated 180,000 tons of stone and rock were required to build the cairn that covers this massive passage grave. The cairn itself is fifty feet high and three hundred feet wide, while the passage is over sixty feet long. At six feet tall, I managed to traverse this passage with only a slight stoop, a far cry from the back crawl at Carrowkeel.

A 'Dolmen,' County Claire, Irish Republic.
A Dolmen is a Passage Grave consisting of several vertical stones capped by one very large horizontal stone. The bodies were buried underneath.

The passage leads to a magnificent central chamber over twenty feet high, with three smaller chambers connected to it. This was a virtual twin of the passage grave on top of the mountain at Carrowkeel—on a much larger scale.

Two of the smaller chambers contain stone basins about four feet wide. The other chamber contains two stone basins, one inside the other. Their purpose is unknown.

One feature that is the exact opposite of the grave on Carrowkeel is the solar orientation of the entrance. It is so situated that on the shortest day of the year (the winter solstice), the rising sun creeps up the passageway, and for a period of fifteen to twenty minutes, it bathes the interior chamber in a golden light.

I wondered if this was an attempt to reassure the population that new life, in the form of crops, would come in the spring. Maybe the Passage Grave was so constructed to point that out new life was possible after death, for those who were interred there.

I was debating these possibilities as I hunched slightly forward to make my way back out into the world.

Duns and Brochs

IF THERE WAS ONE THING that the Celtic people liked to do, it was fight. It was in their nature;it was in their blood. They usually fought against their enemies, and they had many. However, if there happened to be a dearth of enemies, they would often fight amongst themselves.

There are two reasons people fight. The first is defense. You fight to defend yourself, or your honour. You may also fight to defend your family, your friends, or your clan.

The second reason is offense. You fight because you want something. It could be something tangible, such as land, women, possessions, or valuables such as gold and silver. On the other hand it could be to attain something intangible such as pride, or glory.

By and large, Celtic warriors, were on the offense.

On a tribal or clan basis, raids were carried out to establish supremacy over others. In order for a raid to be successful, it would have to be well planned and organized. In order for it to be properly organized, you would need a chain of command. To set up a chain of command, you required a leader, or chief.

(We must keep in mind that in Celtic society, women and men often fought side by side. Many women rose to become not only chiefs, but also 'Warrior-Queens.' The most famous was Boadicea, a red-haired Celtic warrior who led a famous revolt against the Romans in first-century Britain.)

The more desirable attributes the chief possessed, the greater were his chances of staging a successful raid. If he was particularly gifted, and lucky, he might even make it to the ripe old age of forty!

Among the chef's attributes, first and foremost was intelligence. Strength and bravery came second. Courage was another major requirement for any leadership role. In those troubled times, those who led did so by first demonstrating their prowess; no one would follow the chief into battle until he had first proven his own mettle.

The chief also had to be a wise man. He had to know the capabilities, and limitations, of those under his command. He had to be able to judge the ebb and flow of any confrontation, and he had to be able to 'cut and run,' when required.

Within the clan, men usually fought on account of their reputation. Young men fought to build or enhance a reputation, while older men (twenty-five or older) fought to preserve a reputation, often against the challenge of a younger warrior. Insults, either real or perceived, were also fertile ground for fights within the clan.

It is always useful to distinguish between a raid and a battle.

A raid was basically a 'hit and run' attack. You gathered your forces together (whether six or sixty), explained your strategy, invoked the element of surprise, and attacked. You robbed, raped, and pillaged, not necessarily in that order. You took what you could carry and usually made off with the cattle and the horses. If successful, you lived to raid again.

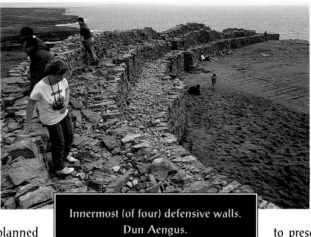

Innermost (of four) defensive walls. Dun Aengus.

Dun Aengus, (Isle of Inishmore, Aran Islands, County Galway, Irish Republic.) Iron-Age Celtic fort on the edge of a 200 ft. cliff. It was the last and strongest of the large Celtic forts built in pre-historic times. There's nothing between it and North America (to the left), except two thousand miles of ocean!

Dun Staigue, County Kerry, Irish Republic.

A battle was quite different. It required a great deal of advance planning and cooperation, because it usually involved the coming together of several clans or tribes. It also meant that the various chiefs would have to agree beforehand on how the spoils of battle would be divided.

Because of the logistics that were required, there was seldom any element of surprise. The enemy knew exactly who you were, and where you were located. They also had ample time to plan their own defense.

Since the battles where conducted on the premise that the 'winner takes all,' at least some of the victors typically remained to take control of the surrounding countryside. Either one clan would secure more territory, or the clans would divide up the territory. This usually required that an

alliance be set up, to ensure that the victors would not immediately start fighting amongst themselves.

The conquerors would lose no time in building some type of fortification to protect themselves, which would also give them a base from which to exercise control over the vanquished.

If the battle involved a successful assault on a previously established fort, then the victors would usually incorporate the undamaged portions of the stronghold into their own defensive strategy.

In order to defend themselves, the early Celts in Scotland and Ireland devised many original forms of protection. Some were unique to their own area, and are not found in other parts of Britain or on the continent. The

Dun Aileach, County Donegal, Irish Republic.

most extraordinary example of this is the 'vitrified fort,' the stone walls of which were fused together by the use of fire.

Another original design, not found anywhere else in the world, is the 'broch,' a massive, circular, stone tower. Also known as a 'dun' (Gaelic for fort), more than five hundred were built in the north of Scotland, the Orkney and Shetland islands, and in the Hebrides. Virtually all are located on the coast or on islands, which seems to indicate that they were built to offer protection from a seaborne assault.

Built sometime between 200 B.C. and 300 A.D., their origin and purpose remains somewhat of a mystery. It is obvious to anyone that they were built for defense, as a place of refuge in time of attack. However, there are no wells located within these structures and most do not have

any source of freshwater within a reasonable distance. It appears that they were designed for short-term use, in order to protect from a raid.

We are still not certain just whom they were built to defend against. Some archaeologists think that because they are only found in the northern part of the British Isles, they must have been built to ward off attacks from Scandinavia.

Although the broch building era was long before the time of the Viking invasions, we do know that the Scandinavians of that period were able seafarers, quite capable of mounting raids on the north of Scotland. If so, were they looking for slaves, booty, or both?

Another theory states that they were built because of raids from the south. Increasing pressure from migrating tribes, especially after the Roman invasion of Britain, may have led the local inhabitants to build these defensive bastions.

There is also the possibility, given the warlike nature of the early Celts, that they were built to protect themselves from themselves! With increasing clan populations, and nowhere else to migrate, local clans may have set out to dominate their neighbours.

Be that as it may, the brochs are formidable defensive positions, as was readily apparent when I visited one of the largest. Dun Carloway (Carloway's Fort), located on the island of Lewis, is the best preserved broch in the Outer Hebrides.

Standing thirty feet high, with a diameter of forty-seven feet, it has 'double' walls that are twelve feet thick at ground level. The inner wall stands vertically, while the outer wall slopes inward. Open spaces, or galleries, within the walls were used for both storage and shelter, and are connected by stone stairs.

There is only one entrance, three feet high and three feet wide. The entrance was sealed with a heavy wooden door, and reinforced with iron rods. This made it very easy to defend since only one person, bent over, could enter at a time, if the door was breached.

Although there are no brochs in Ireland, these Celtic cousins were no slouches when it came to protecting themselves. The most basic form of defence was the 'rath,'

Dun Aileach, on hill top, with Roman Catholic church in a lower meadow. Both are circular in form. County Donegal, Irish Republic.

or ring-fort. It consisted of a circular wall of earth with a wooden palisade on top. Thatched buildings were then built inside the circular wall.

An advance on this was the 'crannog,' or lake-dwelling. This was a small artificial island built in the middle of a small lake, or lagoon. The base was built of logs, stones, and peat. Several small thatched dwellings were located behind a timber palisade on top. Only the inhabitants knew the location of the underwater stepping stones, which were used to connect the crannog to the mainland.

Chiefs and their extended families, usually had more impressive stone fortifications, which were circular in shape. Developed independently of the Scottish broch, these 'duns' were seldom more than twenty feet high, but could range up to one hundred feet in diameter. During times of danger, the chief would invite his kinsmen to take shelter within the walls. Dun Staigue (Staigue's Fort), in the County of Kerry, is one of the finest examples still standing.

Then there is 'Dun Aengus' (Angus's Fort), located on the island of Inishmore in the Aran Islands, County Galway. Built in the first century A.D., and considered to be the finest prehistoric fort in all of western Europe, it is strategically located on the edge of a sheer, two hundred foot cliff.

I have to take my hat off to the unknown engineering genius who planned this awesome defensive position. Not satisfied with one twelve foot thick semi-circular stone wall, he went ahead and built three more. Each successive wall enclosed a larger area, with the outermost encompassing a total of eleven acres!

Outside all of this, he then put in place a fifty foot wide band of vertical limestone pillars. Comprised of thousands of broken and jagged pieces of stone, it was designed to break up the charge of an attacking force, much in the manner of a modern 'tank trap.'

Inishmore is the largest of the three islands that make up the Aran Group, off the west coast of Ireland. Nine miles long, and only two miles wide, it is separated from the Galway mainland by six miles of ocean.

The entire west side of the island is a continuous line of near vertical cliffs, rising to their greatest height at Dun Aengus. Battered, in the autumn and winter months, by mountainous waves, there is nothing between these cliffs and North America except two thousand miles of ocean.

As I stood close to the edge of the cliff at Dun Aengus, and looked out across the vast, empty, reaches of the North

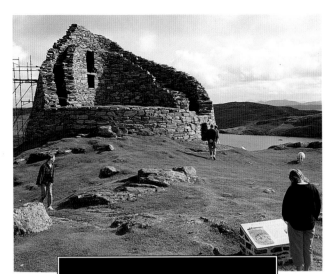

Dun Carloway Broch, Isle of Lewis, Outer Hebrides. This view shows double–walled construction, with galleries within the walls.

Atlantic, the true significance of its marvellous defensive position dawned on me.

Two thousand years ago, this was the end of the known world. There was nowhere left to go.

Was this fact uppermost in the mind of the Celtic genius who designed Dun Aengus? Did he try to construct the ultimate fortification, secure in the knowledge that this was the end of the line, the last possible refuge?

It could be that his Celtic ancestors, over the preceding generations, had been gradually pushed farther and farther to the west, landing them on this final patch of island.

This unknown master builder may have even been the first Celtic leader to reach this point, the western extremity of the European continent.

If so, he would have realized that other Celtic tribes would surely follow.

So he, and his people, built Dun Aengus. On the edge of the cliff, with their backs to the sea.

And waited.

Skellig Michael

A N INCREDIBLE, IMPOSSIBLE, mad place. I tell you the thing does not belong to any world that you and I have lived and worked in; it is part of our dream world."

When George Bernard Shaw wrote these words, back in 1910, he had just returned from a visit to one of the most remarkable and best preserved archaeological sites in the British Isles. Situated on a narrow ledge, six hundred feet above the water, the little monastery remains virtually the same as when it was first built, more than 1,400 years ago. Perched on a spectacular pinnacle of rock known as Skellig Michael, it is located eight miles out in the ocean, off County Kerry in south-west Ireland.

Dedicated to the Archangel Michael, this location equals, if not surpasses, the sites of the other two great monastic centres in western Europe that were also built in his honour: Mont St. Michel in Normandy (France) and St. Michael's Mount in Cornwall (England).

Following St. Patrick's introduction of Christianity into Ireland in the first half of the fifth century, the Irish Church pretty well went its own way. The Irish form of Christianity was very conservative and was to remain so up until the twelfth century. The ecclesiastical organization of the Irish Church also differed in many ways from the Roman system.

In the Roman system a region was divided up into a number of 'diocese,' each under the control of a bishop. In Celtic Ireland, on the other hand, there was a network of monasteries, each under the rule of an abbot.

Under the Irish monastic system, with its emphasis on learning and culture, the benefits of civilization were preserved during that period of time known as the Dark Ages. During the five centuries between the fall of the Roman Empire in 476 A.D. and the beginning of the tenth century, the Irish monasteries flourished on a scale never seen before or since.

The men and women who followed this ascetic lifestyle committed themselves to a life of self-denial and severe self-discipline, refraining as much as possible from all pleasures and worldly comforts. They believed that in order to know God, they had to combine extreme devotion, and an unshakeable faith, with this particular lifestyle.

Although they deemed it necessary to discipline the body by means of such hardships, the same was not true of the mind. In actual fact, the severe monastic way of life seems to have had the opposite effect on the mental alertness and creativity of the monks and nuns.

Freed from all need to worry about personal matters, the monks were free to devote most of their time to artistic and literary pursuits. While the rest of Europe and the British Isles were reeling under the attacks of various barbarian tribes, the Irish monasteries reached an unparalleled level of culture and sophistication, the likes of which has not been seen since.

There is no better way to re-capture the spirit of this ascetic world, and the conservative nature of the early Celtic Church, than to make a modern-day pilgrimage to this holy shrine.

In the summer of 1989 I was finally able to scramble ashore on Skellig Michael, after a rough two-hour crossing in a small fishing boat. On two previous trips to Ireland weather conditions had prevented me from making a landing, in spite of the considerable skills of the local boatmen.

The boat had been waiting for us at a wharf in the little village of Portmagee, on the Iveragh Peninsula in County Kerry. Approximately thirty-two feet long, with benches along the sides and across the stern, it had obvious-

Little Skellig, from the lighthouse road.

ly been fitted out to take a dozen or so passengers on short day trips.

Aside from a small cabin only big enough for the two crew members, the seaworthy little craft was open for the rest of its length. There were no toilet facilities and, surprisingly, no life jackets for the sixteen passengers. I was the only North American. Along with six members of an Irish family, we had four Italians, two Norwegians, and three visitors from France. For the last half of the two-hour journey I sat with my back to the bow. Snuggled into the makeshift shelter provided by the left side of my body, a ten-year old Irish girl tried to make the best of a distinctly unpleasant ride.

Fiona had started to show signs of seasickness not long after we left the confines of the narrow channel and slipped out into the full reach of the North Atlantic. The wind off the open ocean buffeted us and for a short period of time we were tossed about at random as conflicting tides and currents collided at the junction of harbour and ocean.

Once away from the riptide near the shore, things calmed down a bit and we settled into a regular routine of meeting, and surmounting, the ocean swells that lunged at us from the south-west. With the two crewmen snug inside the tiny cabin, we were left at the mercy of the elements. The darkened sky had grown menacing.

Several of the passengers took out rain capes and rain hats while others hastily put away their cameras and binoculars. Fiona's mother reached deep into a cavernous knapsack and distributed thick sweaters to her children, while her husband put an extra blanket around the baby that snuggled in his arms.

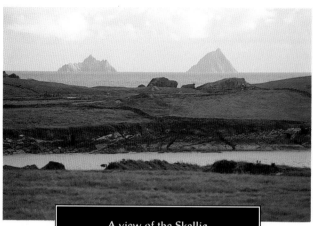

A view of the Skellig (Little Skellig and Great Skellig) taken from the mainland. They are located approximately eight miles off the coast of county Kerry in south-west Ireland.

For a short while I held the sleeping child, while the father put on a thick woolen sweater and checked on the condition of the rest of his family. Most had started to show increasing signs of seasickness, as were several others of the passengers.

While attending university in Nova Scotia, I had spent five summers working at sea off the coast of Newfoundland and Labrador. As a member of the Steward's Department with Marine Atlantic I had gained first-hand knowledge, on more than one occasion, of just how uncomfortable it was to be seasick.

When it became evident that I still had my sea legs, I offered to entertain Fiona in the hopes that it might distract her from the nature of her misery.

In a voice loud enough for all to hear, I offered the following advice:

"Don't look at the waves or down at the water. Look off in the distance and keep your eyes on the horizon."

It was an old seaman's trick and, as is usually the case in such circumstances, it worked. Stories about Canada and the Royal Canadian Mounties also helped to keep Fiona's mind occupied.

We could not see where we were going but we were able to keep watching the coastline of County Kerry as it began to recede. Although at times we could plainly see rain squalls dancing in the distance, aside from a few sporadic drops, we remained reasonably snug and dry.

We were all caught in our own little world—at the mercy of sea and sky. For myself, there was plenty of time to reflect on the nature of the adventure that lay ahead. As

Great Skellig

Fiona dozed on my shoulder, my many readings flashed through my mind.

Skellig Michael is the larger of two islands, which is collectively known as The Skelligs. In Irish Gaelic the name means 'Rock Splinter.' The smaller of the two, and separated from its larger and more famous brother by one mile of water, is known as Little Skellig. The earliest reference to these islands comes from an ancient Irish journal which makes mention of a shipwreck that occurred on the Great Skellig, sometime around 1400 B.C.

With the coming of Irish Christianity came the founding of a monastery on this isolated and imposing rock spire. It is not known who the founder of this religious settlement was, but legend indicates a certain St. Finian.

Sometime early in the sixth century, he and some other monks journeyed to Skellig Michael. Approximately six hundred feet above the waves, on the island's only patch of level ground, they built a little monastic community consisting of six beehive-shaped stone huts, a small church, and a stone oratory with a barrel-vault roof.

(Archaeological evidence has verified that the monastery was probably built early in the sixth century.)

It was sacked by the Vikings on several occasions in the ninth and tenth centuries, yet it remained occupied by monks until the end of the Middle Ages. Religious pilgrimage continued until the middle of the last century. Today, in the summer season, local fishermen take tourists out to the island daily, depending on weather conditions.

After about an hour and a half, the mesmerizing rise and fall of successive ocean swells gave way to a gentle rocking to and fro. The captain had throttled back the engine, as we were now on the lee side of Little Skellig. As we marvelled at the fantastic diversity of bird life on this little sanctuary, Skellig Michael itself came into view.

I have never experienced anything to equal the dramatic effect of that moment. The magnitude of what lay before us, the sheer size and massive bulk of this rock pinnacle, thrusting itself 714 feet straight up out of the ocean, left us staring in silence. Massive! Majestic! Awe-inspiring!

Immediately, George Bernard Shaw's famous quote came to mind.

"An incredible, impossible, mad place. I tell you the thing does not belong to any world that you and I have lived and worked in; it is part of our dream world."

For the rest of the journey we watched in wonder as the Great Skellig loomed closer and closer. Cameras clicked and binoculars made the rounds. No one was left out.

The captain invited me into the cramped confines of the little cabin to observe our approach to the landing spot,

An authentic, 1,400 year old, stairway to heaven. Approximately 500 stone steps, put in place by the original monks, lead to a narrow crest between the two peaks known as 'Christ's Saddle.' Fiona, my little red-haired friend, is on the left along with her father, her sister, and her baby brother.

in Blind Man's Cove on the east side of the island. Pointing to the depth finder, he indicated that the sheer, nearly vertical, walls of the Great Skellig extended underwater to a depth of over 250 feet. That meant that a total of almost one thousand feet of vertical rock pinnacle rose from the floor of the Continental Shelf. Amazing!

There are three possible landing sites on Great Skellig, only one of which can be used by visiting tourists. All three consist of stone steps cut into the near-vertical rock face, and run from sea level to the site of the monastery, six hundred feet above. All three were used by the original inhabitants of the monastery, depending on the wind, tide, and wave conditions.

From the spot where we were put ashore, a narrow rock pathway followed the contours of the island and led us ever upward. It was blasted out of the sheer rock face, in 1826, by a group of engineers who built two lighthouses on the island; one at 175 feet above sea level and another at 375 feet above sea level.

After about a quarter mile, we began the real ascent to the monastery when we approached another of the original stairways that leads up from the water below. It was a slow and deliberate climb up the six hundred stone steps that

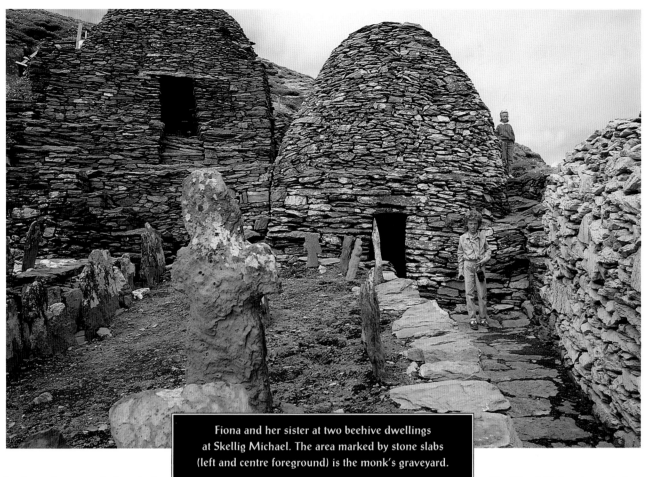

Fiona and her sister at two beehive dwellings
at Skellig Michael. The area marked by stone slabs
(left and centre foreground) is the monk's graveyard.

took us to a spot, located between the twin peaks of the island, known as Christ's Saddle. From here, another one hundred stone steps led up to the monastery itself.

A tunnel in a retaining wall led to the actual terrace on which the monastery stood. Emerging from that tunnel, I stepped back in time to confront a religious site that has remained virtually unchanged for almost 1,400 years.

Its remote location, and a frost-free climate courtesy of the Gulf Stream, account for the excellent state of preservation of the entire settlement. I had first been told of the monastic remains atop Skellig Michael while visiting the holy island of Iona off the west coast of Scotland. Unlike Iona, where nothing remains of the original monastery that was founded by the Irish monk St. Columba in AD 563,

Skellig Michael contains original buildings, which are basically unchanged.

Within an hour of our arrival other fishing boats had brought more visitors. Because of ongoing archaeological work at the site, we were ushered into the walled compound in groups of about twenty.

The buildings that had been used for living quarters were constructed of flat stones placed together, without mortar, in such a manner that they have remained weatherproof for well over a millennium.

The technique, known as 'Corbelling,' makes it possible to construct a dome by laying horizontal rings of stone which decrease in diameter towards the top of the structure, thus overlapping on each course. The gap left at the top of the dome is then closed by a single stone.

The second and highest of the two peaks on Skellig Michael, 714 feet above sea level. There's a prehistoric 'standing stone' on top, with incised Celtic Cross. Medieval pilgrims, after visiting the monastery, would climb to the top and kiss the Cross, thus proving their piety!

Known as 'beehive huts,' because of their resemblance to an old–fashioned beehive, they have been in use since prehistoric times and are often found in Celtic areas.

With no windows, and doorways only four feet high, their cramped interiors offered little in the way of material comforts. This was, however, appropriate since the men who came here to seek spiritual enlightenment had, by so doing, given up the need for comfortable surroundings which they had left behind on the mainland.

After leaving the compound, I sat with several others on the edge of a small terrace. Five hundred feet below, the boats that brought us looked like so many children's toys while gannets, puffins, and kittiwakes engaged in graceful flights of fancy above and around us. An Italian couple who knew very little English shared their lunch with me, an act of kindness that was very much appreciated as I had neglected to bring one of my own.

I later climbed part way to the top of the highest peak on the island (714 feet) and from that vantage point was able to look down on one of the two lighthouses that had been built in 1826. Off to my right stretched the vast expanse of the North Atlantic. There was nothing between me and Nova Scotia, except two thousand miles of open ocean.

In brilliant sunshine I sat and tried to imagine what life must have been like for these men of God, especially in the winter months when they were entirely cut off from the outside world. Although there is never any ice or snow at the Skellings, the wind blows constantly and the ocean is always turbulent.

Winter gales frequently send waves pounding up to the two hundred foot mark. On December 27, 1955, the men at the lower lighthouse reported that a wave had broken the glass of the lighthouse lantern, and extinguished the light, wreaking extensive damage and washing one of the staff down the lighthouse stairs. All this at a height of 175 feet above sea level!

Directly below, in a scene that had been repeated countless times over the last one thousand years, small groups of individuals made their way up and down the stone steps running from Christ's Saddle to the monastery plateau. Over the last millennium, Skellig Michael had developed a reputation as one of the holiest pilgrimage sites in Western

Descending 100 stone steps from monastery plateau to Christ's Saddle.

Europe during the relatively calm summer months.

After three hours ashore we reluctantly returned to our little vessel. We were, after all, latter day pilgrims who had been just as moved by our visit to this desolate, yet breathtakingly beautiful place of worship, as any who had come before.

We sat in silence as we backed away from the jetty and headed out into a strong late afternoon swell. Fiona, who had remained in my care while ashore, had found her sea legs and was now quite comfortable despite the often erratic movements of the small boat. As Skellig Michael receded, we resumed our conversation.

"Are there places like Skellig in Canada?"

"No. I'm afraid not."

"Do you think that the Holy Men ever get tired of talking to God?"

Two hours was not nearly enough time to answer the questions of this little Irish lady, who spent the last portion of our remarkable journey, asleep on my shoulder.

Fingal's Cave
Isle of Staffa

CAVES, LIKE CASTLES, hold an eternal fascination for most of us. Even people who would never dare enter a cave—especially alone—will stand around outside the entrance, seemingly enthralled by the possibilities of just what might be found inside.

There is in all of us a fear and fascination with caves that takes us back to the time of our earliest ancestors, a prehistoric time when access to a cave often meant the difference between life and death. A cave was a place of refuge from the often violent and deadly world. It also served as a shelter from the elements, a dwelling, a storehouse, a communal gathering spot, and even a place of burial.

When societies became more settled and civilized, and it was no longer necessary to rely so heavily on caves, they often became places of religious significance or centres of superstition. Even today, as we stand on the threshold of the twenty-first century, unusual and distinctive caves remain one of the premier tourist attractions in those parts of the world fortunate enough to have them.

So it is with Fingal's Cave, on the Isle of Staffa. One of the most fascinating islands in the Inner Hebrides, and one of the most unusual in the Western Hemisphere, Staffa is world famous for its extraordinary caves and its basaltic (lava) formations.

Covering a total area of just seventy-one acres, the Isle of Staffa is about three-quarters of a mile long and a quarter of a mile wide. Its highest point, located at its southern end, is 135 feet above sea level. The island has been uninhabited for the past two centuries.

A rich pasture covers the entire surface of the treeless island which, for the most part, consists of an uneven plateau. Since the coastline is composed almost entirely of shoreless cliffs, there are only a few spots where a boat can land. Depending on the tide and weather conditions, it is possible to come ashore at the south-east end of the island, not far from the island's only serviceable well.

What is now Staffa came into existence when the nearby island of Mull was the centre of colossal volcanic activity. This took place about forty million years ago.

Staffa is Norse for 'Stave Island,' for the Norsemen (Vikings) built their houses of tree trunks set vertically to resemble the island's basaltic columns. The remarkable hexagonal columns of basalt, which give the look of a rugged stockade to Staffa's southern and western cliffs, were formed by a particular pattern in the cooling of molten lava.

Its coastline is penetrated by several caves, the most famous of which takes its name from the third-century Irish hero, 'Fionn MacCoull.' Known in Scotland as 'Fingal,' he is said to have used the cave as a hideout while defending the Hebrides against early pirates. He died in battle in 283 A.D.

Fingal's Cave is unique. At its entrance, smooth black columns of basalt rise out of the sea like the pipes of some great organ. The interior is lined with black, hexagonal columns which, on the left wall, rise forty feet in perfect symmetry. From an opening sixty feet wide and sixty-five feet high, the passage gradually narrows until it is but six feet wide and ten feet high. At this point you are two hundred and thirty feet from daylight.

Above the entrance there is a thirty foot expanse of cliff face. Thus, from sea level to skyline, Fingal's Cave rises nearly one hundred feet in architectural magnitude and magnificence, all in stone. It's a display of molten lava from forty million years ago, frozen in a fantastic display of the Creator's whimsy.

View from approximately 50 to 60 feet inside
Fingal's Cave, Isle of Staffa.

Fingal's Cave, Isle of Staffa.

People come from all parts of the world to see Fingal's Cave, and experienced travellers declare that nowhere else in the world have they seen anything quite as splendid. Although many caves are larger and many cliffs are higher, none of them occur in a setting quite so solemn, so wondrous, and so inspiring.

The cave's original Gaelic name is 'An Uamh Ehirn' (The Musical Cave), from the sounds of the sea echoing through its depths. In storm conditions the pressure of the sea against the cave mouth creates a loud, compressed, booming noise. It was probably this sound that inspired the young German composer, Felix Mendelssohn, to write 'Fingal's Cave Overture' after a visit. He wrote to his sister: "It was like the interior of a gigantic organ for the winds and waves to play on."

One of the first published references to Staffa appeared in an early guide book to Scotland that was printed in 1775. In it a Mr. Pennant, who was not able to come ashore, reported: "Everyone was up and in motion before the break of day. We arrived at the entrance to the cave at first light, where we were struck with a scene of magnificence which far exceeded our expectations. Compared to this, what are the cathedrals or the palaces built by men!"

In 1818 Staffa overwhelmed the great English poet John Keats. "I am puzzled how to give an idea of Staffa," he wrote. "For solemnity and grandeur it far surpasses the finest cathedrals. It is impossible to describe it!"

When in 1847, Queen Victoria and Prince Albert arrived on the Royal Yacht, the sea was calm enough for them to row into the cave itself, in a small boat.

Having just descended, by means of the narrow gully
at top left, from the plateau to sea level.

I was not quite so lucky. It took me three days to reach the island. Although located only six miles from the Isle of Iona, the journey to Staffa involves crossing a dangerous stretch of water in a small open boat.

The first day it was so windy that no boats left the safety of the little harbour on Iona. The second day, we actually made it about a mile from the wharf before the owner of the boat wisely decided to turn back. On the third day we were successful.

The converted fishing boat was not very large, at twenty feet long and eight feet wide. It was completely open to the elements, with an engine compartment in the middle of the boat and some rudimentary seats placed along both sides.

We had each paid twenty dollars to make the crossing, which took about one hour. We left at ten in the morning under dull skies, with a few drops of rain making dancing patterns on the water's surface. In addition to myself, we had a retired couple from Glasgow, two young women from a college in England, and a couple from Wales with their young son.

After an uneventful crossing we were all put ashore with explicit instructions to be back at this same location by three in the afternoon. This would give us about four hours on Staffa.

It took a short while to walk across the plateau that makes up the surface of the island. We walked uphill for most of the distance, following the island's steady increase in height as we moved south toward the caves. Keeping to the outline of a path, we soon arrived at a rough-hewn stairway, which had been carved from the rock. This enabled us to carefully descend approximately one hundred feet to sea level.

Then the magic began. We walked on what appeared to be black, sawed-off tree stumps, most of which were six or eight sided. The stumps were intricately interwoven, with no spaces between any of them. Actually, we were walking on the tops of basaltic columns, hardened pillars of lava, from a primeval volcanic eruption that happened forty million years ago!

On my left, the tops of the basaltic pillars extended to the edge of the water, about twenty feet away. On my immediate right, close enough to touch, the black pillars surged skyward for a good fifty or sixty feet. After about three hundred feet of stepping from pillar to pillar, I rounded a corner and stared straight into the depths of Fingal's Cave.

There, directly in front of me, was the truly massive entrance to this fantastic cavern. Even though the cave had been directly in front of us as we approached by boat, I was totally unprepared for what I was about to see.

The sound of waves breaking somewhere inside was mingled with the cries of sea birds, some of whom flew directly into the cave and disappeared into the black void.

Causeway leading to the entrance to Fingal's Cave, Isle of Staffa.

The vertical rock pillars that framed the opening did indeed give the impression of looking directly into the interior of some gigantic pipe organ. In spite of all that I had read about Fingal's Cave, I was still caught off guard by the magnitude of what lay ahead.

Despite the cautions of my fellow travellers, I set off to venture inside. I pointed out to my party that Nova Scotia was approximately two thousand miles due west. I had not crossed the Atlantic Ocean and travelled across England, Wales, and Lowland Scotland by motorcycle, to stop at the entrance to Fingal's Cove.

I knew from my readings that there was a ledge on the right hand side, about two feet wide and twenty feet up, that extends into the depths of the cavern. I also knew that a little effort and some climbing would take me to the back of the cave, a distance of 230 feet. The worst that could happen, I reassured them, was that I would lose my footing and fall into the water inside the cave, and I was confident that my swimming ability was sufficient to enable me to swim back out.

Leaving my expensive camera and lenses outside, I stuffed a simple point-and-shoot camera into the pocket of my leather motorcycle jacket, climbed to the ledge, and set off into the darkness.

Pillars and Posts make up the causeway to Fingal's Cave.

The ledge that I was walking on varied in width from one foot, at its most narrow point, to about four feet at others. It was actually quite bright, once my eyes adjusted to the diminished light that was available. I was walking on the tops of the basaltic (lava) columns, at a distance that ranged from six to twelve feet above the water level.

With my right hand, I gripped the vertical columns that formed the wall on this side of the cavern. On the far side, the vertical columns extended in an unbroken line from the roof to deep below water level.

At about the halfway point in my excursion I stopped, turned, and very carefully placed my back snug up against the wall. I swept my eyes over all that lay before me.

To my left, the light from the entrance was beginning to lose its brilliance while, off to the right, it was just possible to make out the innermost features of this splendid cavern. Overhead, the vertical columns curved inwards, in the form of an arch. Below, and just barely visible, I could make out the movement of the waves. I was to find out later that the water at this distance from the entrance was about forty feet deep.

After shouting to my friends outside, and assuring them that everything was O.K., I turned carefully to my right and continued on. I had brought a flashlight with me, but did not need it. I could now feel the dampness in the air and I became aware that the temperature had dropped quite a few degrees. Happily, I had worn my leather jacket over a heavy wool shirt.

The ledge started to narrow and I soon found myself approaching the back of the cave. The going got a little dif-

The entrance to Fingal's Cave, Isle of Staffa.

ficult, but I was able to scramble the last few yards and then, suddenly, I could go no further.

I turned around slowly, taking time to regain my breath. As I took in my immediate surroundings, I realized that it was possible for me to sit down. It was only then that I felt the gentle pumping action of the air, a pumping action that I soon realized was tied in with the motion of the waves.

As the waves made their way to the back of the cavern they compressed the air. As they retreated, the air was drawn out again. It produced an uncanny sensation, which literally took my breath away!

Sitting in the back of Fingal's Cave, 230 feet from the entrance, I became keenly aware that the trials and tribulations of the world were quite far away. Insulated as I was from any vision of the outside world, save for the shaft of light at the entrance, I fell into a contemplative mood.

Historical records indicate that the early monks on Iona considered Fingal's Cave to be a rather special example of the creative power of God. Its unique configuration, combined with its remote location, made it an ideal site for those who wished to seclude themselves in meditation. The records also indicate that several monks who tried to ride out bad weather inside the cave had an early encounter with their maker!

"Hello! Hello! Are you there, Canada?"

"Yes, I'm at the back."

"Are you O.K.?"

"Yes, I'm fine."

"You've been inside almost an hour. Time to get back to the boat!"

"O.K., I'm on my way. Be there soon."

I was surprised to learn how much time had passed. Our boat was due to return within the hour and the others were obviously reluctant to start the trek back to the landing site while I was still inside the cave.

The return to the entrance was relatively easy, taking only half the time as the way in. At more than one point I had to stop and pause for a few minutes, to allow my eyes to adjust to the rapidly increasing intensity of light. I also noticed the temperature increase, as I drew closer to the entrance. Suddenly, I was standing in brilliant sunshine.

Willing hands helped me down from the ledge. The air was full of questions.

"How far did you get?"

"What did you see?"

"Was it cold?"

"Were you scared?"

"Any bats?"

"No bats!"

After a few minutes interlude, we retraced our steps along the side of the island, climbed the terraced stone path to the grassy plateau, and set off in the direction of the landing spot. Within half an hour we were back at the little wharf. Our boat had arrived about ten minutes earlier.

On hearing of my jaunt to the back of the cave, the captain decided to take us much closer to shore than he normally would on the ride back. As we drew even with the entrance, he throttled back the engine. When Fingal's Cave came into full view, he threw the transmission into neutral and we came to a stop.

Rocking gently to and fro, we sat and stared in silence. A religious silence. The kind you experience when you know that you are in the presence of something quite extraordinary.

Make no mistake about it. This tiny little island, like the slightly larger island of Iona itself, is a very holy place. The presence of God was overpowering.

No one spoke. No one wanted to leave.

The magic of the moment, and I have no doubt that that's what it was, was rudely shattered as the engine roared back to life. We turned away from Fingal's Cave and pointed our bow in the direction of Iona, six miles away. As Staffa receded in the distance, we slipped quickly across the waves.

Castles and Towers
Fortified Dwellings

ALTHOUGH THE HIGHLANDS and Islands of Scotland saw periods of relative prosperity during the late Middle Ages (1000 to 1450 A.D.), we know that it was also a time of intense feuding between the clans. The numerous castles and fortified tower houses that were constructed during this period bear ample witness to these seemingly contradictory statements.

While most of these buildings were erected on the ruins of earlier fortifications, some dating back to prehistoric times, the rise of the castle and fortified tower house as we know it would not have been possible without substantial amounts of money, manpower, and often times an amazing degree of engineering know-how.

The west coast was one of the last areas in Scotland to come under royal authority, beginning in the thirteenth century. Most, if not all, of the fortified buildings constructed during that period were built with some measure of royal assistance. If not royal, then at least with the help of nobility.

The clan chief would provide the manpower and raw materials while the royal personage provided most of the money and the engineering expertise.

Although there were many variations, the fortified dwellings of Scotland can be loosely classified as either 'castles of enclosure' or 'fortified tower houses.'

In the case of the former, a stone wall, called a 'curtain wall,' encloses a courtyard. Within this courtyard can be found timber buildings, either free-standing, or flush against the stone wall.

In pre-historic times, the wall was typically made of earth.

Originally, 'fortified tower houses' were simple stone towers, rectangular in shape and about four stories high. The first floor was normally a cellar, used for storage and supplies. On the second level was the main hall which was used for dining, entertainment, and relaxation. The two upper floors housed the sleeping quarters.

Fortified tower houses are found in all parts of the Highlands and Islands. They are either found in isolation or as additions to earlier castles of enclosure, in which case they were built to provide greater comfort and security.

Of the many hundreds of fortified dwellings to be found throughout the Highlands and Islands of Scotland, two distinguished themselves to me in my travels. Duart Castle, in the Inner Hebrides, is the ancestral home of the Clan MacLean while Kisimul Castle, in the Outer Hebrides, is the ancestral home of the Clan MacNeil. Both of them played pivotal roles in the history of Scotland.

The outstanding location of Duart Castle, standing high on a point of land on the Isle of Mull, has helped to make it one of the most impressive fortifications in all of Scotland. It dominates the southern approach to the Sound

Duart Castle from the Sound of Mull.

The 'keep,' Duart Castle, located about 80 feet above the water. Notice the virtual absence of windows. Those that do exist are small enough to admit a little light, and to allow the defenders to shoot arrows out with little chance of being hit themselves.

of Mull and is visible to every visitor to Mull and the Southern Hebrides.

Protected by a great windowless wall, thirty feet high and almost ten feet thick, it is every inch of what a fortress should be. When seen from the sea, it forms an integral part of the great cliff it crowns and dominates.

The original fortification was a simple, rectangular, castle of enclosure, probably built by the MacDougall Clan early in the thirteenth century. The unusually massive tower house, a later addition for increased security, measures sixty-three feet by forty-six feet with walls nearly fif-teen feet thick. This was the last refuge for those in the castle, if the outer defensive walls were to be breached. It dates from the late fourteenth century, by which time the building had fallen into Clan MacLean hands.

Duart Castle, home of the Chiefs of the MacLeans of Duart, was built with one purpose in mind: to keep people out. Unlike those who would later build extravagant castles, in a vain attempt to display their wealth, the Duart MacLeans were extremely practical. Their primary intent was to ensure that everyone knew exactly who was boss, and where that boss lived.

Kisimul Castle, Castlebay, Isle of Barra.

The name "Duart" is from the Gaelic "Dubh Ard" and translates as "The Black Height," a reference to the cliff on which the castle stands. Like most strongholds of the Scottish clans, it must have seen much good and evil. Yet, if approached from its landward side on a cold and wet day, it is the dark side of Duart that registers with the mind.

Duart Castle and the MacLeans who occupied it down through the centuries bring into sharp focus the best and the worst of our Celtic heritage.

On one hand it reinforces the image of our Celtic ancestors as a group of brazen barbarians, intent on nothing more uplifting than attacking rival clans and stealing their women and their cattle. On the other hand it represents an attempt to bring some order out of the chaotic times in which it was first built and occupied. If this involved the defeat and subjugation of neighbouring clans on neighbouring islands, so be it.

Consider what is going on today in two separate parts of the world. In the former Yugoslavia the demise of communism has resulted in the emergence of ethnic forces (clans) that are evidently intent on the destruction of those who do not fit into a certain ethnic profile. In the East African nation of Somalia there has been a complete breakdown of civil authority. The government has ceased to exist. The mass starvation that we see on nightly television is but one byproduct of a particularly vicious form of inter-tribal (clan) warfare.

Duart Castle was occupied by the MacLeans until the seventeenth century when they were defeated by a rival clan. The castle was later taken over by the English government

View from the ramparts of Kisimul Castle. Village of Castlebay in the background. This lifeboat performs rescues in some of the most dangerous waters around the British Isles.

and used as a barracks until the end of the eighteenth century.

Over the next one hundred years, the castle lay empty and fell into ruin. The roof collapsed and the interior rooms were left open to the elements. At the turn of the last century it was bought by Sir Fitzroy MacLean, twenty-sixth Chief of Clan MacLean, who, with the help of fellow clansmen from around the world, rebuilt the fortress.

Duart Castle has many ties with the Maritime Provinces. On Cape Breton Island, for example, MacLeans of Washabuckt, Christmas Island, Boisdale, and Beaver Cove, are all direct descendants of the MacLeans of Duart. Other descendants are to be found in various parts of Canada, the United States, Australia, and New Zealand.

During the week I spent on the Isle of Mull, I made three visits to Duart Castle. I had been drawn there by the fact that my mother's maiden name was MacLean. The last of these visits was on a cold and damp day, and the intermittent drizzle made it all but impossible to appreciate the surrounding countryside.

The bright side was that, due to the adverse weather conditions, there were no other tourists around. So I had those portions of the castle, that were open to the public, all to myself. I was thus able to leisurely review some of the intriguing stories of Duart Castle, and of the individuals who had once called it home.

The further I probed into its past, the more I saw that the history of the island of Mull, like that of the rest of the

Highlands and Islands of Scotland, was a never-ending story of the warring clans.

For a long time the MacLeans of Duart feuded with a rival branch of their clan, the MacLaines of Loch Buie. (Notice the spelling of both names!) The Loch Buie branch had their own castle, which was much smaller than Duart. Today it lies in ruins. What remains is a tall, gaunt, square

The author and piano, Brodick Castle, Isle of Arran, Inner Hebrides.

tower, roofless and empty, its walls partially clad with ivy.

Well over three hundred years ago it was recorded that 'Big Hector' MacLean of Duart supported Ian 'The Toothless' MacLaine of Loch Buie in putting down a rebellion led by Ian's only son, 'Ewan of the Little Head.'

Ewan had a very misshapen skull due to complications at his birth. He also had the bad luck to lose his head (literally!) in the battle that ensued. For two days his terrified horse, carrying the decapitated Ewan, roamed the hills and glens of Mull. The horse finally collapsed and died from exhaustion, or perhaps fright, and poor Ewan was given a proper, although headless, burial.

His headless spirit, on horseback, is sometimes seen on the Isle of Mull. It is usually interpreted to mean that a direct relative of the Loch Buie Clan Chief is about to die.

Then there is the documented story of Lachlan MacLean of Duart, who lived in the sixteenth century. MacLean was upset with his wife, Lady Catherine Campbell, because she had not provided him with a son. One night he tied her up and rowed her out to a partially submerged rock, about one mile offshore from the castle. He knew that the rock would disappear under several feet of water at high tide. When he looked out the next morning, she was gone. At once, MacLean sent word of her

untimely death to her relatives, the Campbells.

A day or two later, Lachlan MacLean and a large group of his kinsmen arrived at her father's castle with an empty coffin. The mourning widower was at once ushered into the great dining hall and there, waiting for him at the head of the table, sat his wife. Passing fishermen had rescued Lady Catherine shortly before high tide. No word of this was said at the table where MacLean and his retinue were forced to eat. The state of mind in which their guest was obliged to eat his meal must have caused his hosts immense satisfaction. To prolong it further, they allowed him to make his escape. After a discreet interval Lachlan MacLean was murdered in his bed, by his wife's brother, during a visit to Edinburgh!

I had become so absorbed in reading about the MacLeans (and the MacLaines) that suddenly, when I looked up, it was dark. Leaving the small library I quietly made my way from the castle and returned to my motorcycle, without meeting a soul. After putting on my rain gear and helmet, I crossed the deserted parking lot to stand at the edge of the cliff.

Duart Castle loomed over me, dark and silent in the swirling mist. Not a light could be seen. I could hear, but not see, the surf pounding on the rocky shore somewhere below. Off in the distance, about a mile away, a flashing light marked the partially submerged rock where my ancestor had marooned his wife. That fated spot is now considered a serious hazard to ships.

After revving the motorcycle, I took one last glance at Duart before pointing the machine down the road. It was twenty miles to my bed and breakfast. The miserable dri-

External view of Brodick Castle. Notice the windows! Its 'keep,' at rear left, was built for defense like those of Duart and Kisimul. Later additions to the castle were built more for display and to show off the wealth of the clan chief and his family.

ving conditions, on one of the most desolate roads in all of Scotland, somehow felt right. Today, I still refer to a cold, wet, miserable night as a 'Duart Night.'

Kisimul Castle, on the Isle of Barra, is not nearly as large and foreboding as Duart. Yet it has its own rather unique history, being the only castle in the Outer Hebrides.

Its strategic location, on a small island in a corner of Castlebay Harbour, stems from the fact that it stands guard over the first safe anchorage in the Outer Hebrides, to the north of Ireland. Control this bay and you control not only Barra, but all of the surrounding islands as well.

My first glimpse of this small yet intimidating fortification came at about eight in the evening, as the ferry from the mainland swung around some rocky protuberances and sailed into Castlebay Harbour. My first impression was one of surprise and astonishment, for the walls of the castle seem to leap straight out of the sea. Its sudden and dramatic appearance provides a fascinating introduction to the Outer Hebrides.

The journey from the mainland had taken a little over five hours, about the same length of time that it takes to sail from my home town of North Sydney, in Nova Scotia, to Port Aux Basques, Newfoundland. In fact, as we approached the entrance to Castlebay Harbour, I quickly saw a similarity between Barra and Port Aux Basques: no trees!

Both are barren, rocky, and treeless, much as they had been when the glaciers retreated at the end of the last ice age. The entrance to each harbour is dangerous, as there are numerous shoals and hidden rocks. It requires considerable skill and seamanship to bring your vessel safely to shore in both harbours, and the weather, which can turn ugly without warning, plays a major role in determining how closely the ferry sticks to its original timetable.

The Isle of Barra is famous in folklore and legend as the home of the Clan MacNeil, one of the oldest dynasties in all the Hebrides. Some clan historians claim that the MacNeils can be traced back to 'Niall of the Nine Hostages,' a chieftain who ruled in Ireland during the fourth century. Others claim that their distant ancestors were Norse in origin and that the original name was Nilsson.

At this late date in history, it is virtually impossible to determine who is right. What is certain, however, is that Kisimul Castle was the home of the Chiefs of the Clan MacNeil.

Kisimul Castle owed its reputation as one of the most impregnable fortifications in all the Western Isles to a rather unusual geological fact. When primeval forces created a small rocky island a few hundred yards from the inner shore, those same forces also saw fit to provide an underground geological 'pipe' that brings water through the underlying rock strata to a small well on the Island's surface.

Beautiful example of a 'fortified tower house,' without later additions. This tower house is in County Tipperary, Irish Republic.

This gift—a fresh-water well in the midst of a salt-water harbour—made it possible to fortify the small island, safe in the knowledge that the defenders could hold out as long as their food supply would allow.

It is generally accepted that the castle was first constructed sometime in the twelfth or thirteenth century. As was the case with Duart Castle, it had more than likely been built on the ruins of earlier fortifications, dating back to pre-historic times.

In 1795, a devastating fire destroyed all wooden structures within the stone walls, and the castle remained a ruin until 1937, when it was purchased by a certain Robert Lister from Canada. He turned out to be a direct descendant of the last of the old chiefs, Roderick MacNeil. Dubbed 'The General,' MacNeil died in 1863.

The castle was completely restored between 1956 and 1970. This was made possible through donations from MacNeil clansmen from around the world, in addition to substantial contributions from the Scottish government.

The MacNeils of Barra were known far and wide as excellent sailors and navigators, which might naturally be assumed given the location of Barra at the southern tip of the Outer Hebrides. They also earned the reputation of sea-raiders and pirates, and were renowned for living life, short as it might be, to the fullest.

The MacNeil chiefs were not known for their humility. In the sixteenth and seventeenth centuries, it was common practice for an aide to the chief to make the following proclamation from the ramparts of Kisimul Castle: "Hear ye, all ye nations of the world. The Great MacNeil of Barra has finished his evening meal. Ye kings and princes of the nations of the earth may now dine!"

On the day of my visit to Kisimul Castle, I had the good fortune of being alone for the first hour. Without distraction I could examine the eight structures located within the twelve-foot high walls, including a small chapel containing the body of Robert Lister.

A fortified tower house in the county Limerick, Irish Republic.

at the seven foot level. This made it possible to sleep twice as many soldiers in times of attack.

The small dungeon, located at the bottom of the watchtower, was entered by means of a trap door in the floor above. Through this prisoners were lowered, or thrown, to the bottom. The primitive toilet, nothing more than a hole in the floor, was simply flushed out twice a day by the changing tides. The same tidal action was used for other toilets located in the castle.

As I stood alone, on the ramparts of the watchtower, it did not take much imagination to visualize what it must have been like to stand watch, three or four centuries ago, on a cold, wet, dismal winter's night.

The great hall, which is about twenty feet by forty feet, was originally one storey high. The ceiling was later raised to thirteen feet and a 'temporary' floor was installed

That they were hardy men, these defenders of Kisimul, is clear. The Castle has never been taken by force of arms!

The Isle of Eigg

I LL CALL HER SAMANTHA—'Sam' for short— since this was the name she used when we first met. For all I know she might still be living there, under an assumed name, not really trusting new visitors to the island.

At first she was reluctant to tell me much about herself, probably because she was not convinced that I was genuine. Was I really a guidance counsellor/photography instructor from Canada, or was I, in fact, an employee of the British Government? After all, this young lady was on the run, and the authorities were looking for her.

Originally from South Africa, she had entered the British Isles on a six-month tourist visa about four years before we met. After one month in London, she had toured England and Wales before becoming romantically involved with a certain young man in the city of Birmingham.

She moved in with him and they remained together for about a year, before deciding to go their separate ways. By this time, however, the British immigration authorities were looking for her, as well as officials from her own embassy. It seems that governments do not take kindly to people who abuse their tourist visas, or their passports.

Be that as it may, Sam was certainly making it difficult for them. For if you wanted to pick a location in the British Isles in which to hide from someone, you would be hard pressed to find a spot as remote as the small island of Eigg, population seventy-five, in the Inner Hebrides.

Located twelve miles out in the Atlantic, Eigg is one of four small islands that are collectively known as 'The Parish of the Small Isles.' (The others are the isles of Rhum, Muck, and Canna.)

Five miles long and three miles wide, Eigg is one of the most intriguing of all the islands in the Hebrides. Unlike most of the others, it is partially wooded and is actually quite fertile. The mild climate is generally frost-free and allows tropical palms to flourish alongside the local vegetation.

In Gaelic, Eigg means 'notch' or 'hollow.' When looked at from the sea, it does indeed seem as if some pre-historic giant has carved a notch across the center of the island. This notch separates the famous rock formation known as 'An Sgurr' from the rest of the island.

An enormous, hulking mass of pitchstone, An Sgurr presents a formidable appearance, especially when seen from up close. Menacing might be a better word. You get the distinct feeling that this is a lot more than just the largest piece of solid rock in the British Isles.

Rising to a height of 1,289 feet, and surrounded by vertical cliffs on three sides, it exudes an unmistakable aura of danger. On the east face, the cliffs of this miniature mountain reach their maximum height in a fantastic overhanging nose. The base of this basaltic nose is more than five hundred feet above ground level!

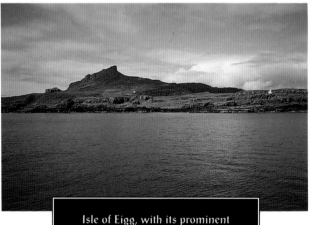

Isle of Eigg, with its prominent and very distinctive rock formation known as 'An Sgurr.'

Frontal view of the peak of An Sgurr, Isle of Eigg.
A prehistoric 'vitrified' fort that is on top, is not visible here.

As if its location and dramatic appearance were not enough, the highest point of An Sgurr displays a perfect example of one of the most fascinating and unexplained riddles in all of Celtic archaeology; a 'vitrified fort.'

Sometime between 500 and 200 B.C., a group of Celtic men climbed to the top of An Sgurr and built a fort. Built of stone and located just above the

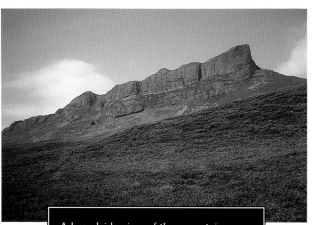

A broadside view of the mountain range known as 'An Sgurr.'

overhanging nose, it is rectangular in form and straddles the summit. With near vertical 1,200–foot cliffs on three sides, it could only be approached from the west, across a narrow ridge of rock. It is considered to have been the most strategically situated Iron Age fort in all the British Isles.

Riddle #1: If the fort could only be approached from one side because of the cliffs, why build four walls when only one (on the west) was necessary?

No one knows how much manpower was required to transport enough stone to the summit to construct the ten to twelve foot thick walls. The type of stone found in the walls is not found on the summit ridge. It came from an area near the base of the mountain.

The pre-historic engineering genius who designed this fort, and presumably supervised its construction, did not construct just ordinary stone walls, as was the custom in other pre-historic societies. (Vitrified forts are unique to Scotland and the Hebrides.)

Instead, he first built a grid of large wooden beams and then fit the stone over and around the grid. This resulted in a reinforced wall that was immensely strong and sturdy.

Riddle #2: Where did the timber for the wooden beams come from, and how was it transported to the summit? The timber did not come from Eigg.

Then came a stroke of genius. When the fort was completed, he set fire to the entire structure. As the fire spread to the timbers that formed the nucleus of the walls, they turned to charcoal and the temperature inside the ramparts reached more than 1,200 degrees Celsius. The stone blocks cracked and melted and the quartz in the rock reverted to the molten state. This process is known as vitrification.

As the fire raged and increased in intensity, fed by enormous drafts of oxygen from the open air, the walls of the fort literally melted together. Streams of molten glass ran down the side of the cliffs and gathered in pools more than a thousand feet below.

Riddle #3: Why vitrify a stone fort that was already virtually impregnable? Its location, and the fact that it could only be approached from one direction, meant that it would have been very easy to defend.

Riddle #4: How was the intense heat generated, and how was it sustained over a long period of time?

It has been estimated that in order to vitrify a stone fort of the size found on An Sgurr, you would need in the vicinity of several hundred tons of wood. A temperature in excess of 1,200 degrees Celsius would then have to be maintained for not less than ten-twelve hours.

Can't be done! Not 1,200 feet up in the air!

As I stood on the vitrified eastern wall of this Iron Age Celtic fort, that was the only conclusion that I, a rational, educated, guidance counsellor, could make.

Where did they get the enormous quantities of wood, and how was it carried to the summit? How was it placed around the outer walls of the fort, walls that perch on the

The author and an Ordnance Survey summit marker on the highest point of An Sgurr, Isle of Eigg. The Cullin Mountains of Rhum are visible on the horizon.

edge of cliffs that are more than 1,200 feet high?

And how was that temperature maintained for such an extended period of time?

What modern science says can't be done, our uncivilized, uneducated Celtic ancestors achieved. This is an intriguing archaeological puzzle that will likely remain unsolved.

It was my desire to examine this vitrified fort that brought me to Eigg in the first place. The day I set out to climb An Sgurr was also the day I met Sam.

In her short stay on Eigg she had become fascinated with the history of this remarkable little island, and over the next three days, she was my guide and resident historian.

The island had always been privately owned, usually by absentee landlords. Up until 1745 it was part of the Clan MacDonald holdings. However, after the Battle of Culloden Moor and the breakup of the clan system, things started to come apart for the tightly-knit little Celtic community on Eigg.

A government survey in 1771 indicated a population of 459: 183 males and 276 females. They appear to have lived quite comfortably. In the summer they fished, herded their cattle, tended their small fertile plots of land, and cut the peat that would keep them snug and warm in the winter.

By the early 1800s, however, the infamous Highland Clearances were under way and the local inhabitants were forced to emigrate in order to make way for more profitable sheep farms. In 1853 all the crofters, with the exception of

Part of 'vitrified' fort, 'lunar' landscape of Isle of Eigg, and Cuillin of Rhum on horizon.

one MacKinnon family, were forced off their land and shipped out for North America. They included MacDonalds, MacKays, MacQuarries, and Campbells.

During the early years of this century the island was sold several times. In the years after the Second World War the younger generation moved to the mainland in search of work, and the fortunes of Eigg slipped to an all-time low. By 1975 the population had fallen to thirty-nine, with only two children attending the local school.

Shortly thereafter, the island was sold to an English businessman from Yorkshire for five hundred thousand dollars. He had come to the Hebrides on vacation and had fallen in love with the Isle of Eigg. Spending large sums of his own money, he has since stabilized the economy and opened up the island for tourists. It was in his recently renovated lodge that Sam worked as a maid.

I was about to walk in to the base of An Sgurr, intending to find an easy route to its summit, when I came across Sam. She offered to take the next day off work in order to lead me to the summit, and suggested I join her for a walk on the beach.

She neglected to mention that in order to reach the beach we would have to descend a narrow path that wound its way down a one hundred–foot cliff. Our descent ended at a cave—Massacre Cave, as it is known. It was the site of the worst atrocity ever recorded in the history of the Hebrides, an event that even today makes the blood run cold.

The incident took place in March, 1577. A group of young men, all members of the MacLeod Clan from the

Pastoral view of one of the Isle of Eigg's
beautiful sandy beaches.

nearby Isle of Skye, landed on Eigg and sexually molested some young MacDonald girls, who had been tending cattle in a pasture.

Before they could escape they were caught, severely beaten, and set adrift to die in their open boat, with their hands tied behind their backs.

Fortunately for them, the currents carried the small boat back to Skye, where they were found several days later on a deserted beach.

Unfortunately for the inhabitants of Eigg, the Chief of the Clan MacLeod was so incensed by the attack on his men that he vowed revenge. He sent out word to his clansmen and a few days later, several hundred armed men set sail for Eigg.

When word of this impending attack reached Eigg, the entire population made their way to this cave, bringing supplies of food and water with them. Everyone, that is, except a very sick, old woman, who was not able to be moved, and a boatload of young men who were away in Glasgow.

The MacLeods landed and roamed over the entire island looking for retribution. They found the old woman, and, in a compassionate moment that was unusual for the clan wars of that time, they spared her life.

For three days they remained on the island. Frustrated at not finding anyone, and believing that the population had fled to the mainland, they set fire to whatever dwellings they could find and killed all domestic animals.

Fields of heather, Isle of Eigg.

They were just getting ready to leave when one of them happened to notice some footprints in the snow that had just fallen the previous night. They were the footprints of a MacDonald scout, who had been sent from the cave in order to see if the coast was clear.

The MacLeods followed the tracks back to the cave, and to its hidden entrance. When the people inside refused to send out the young men who had defended the girls, the Chief sent his men to gather driftwood that had washed up on the beach. They then piled the timber over the entrance, and set it afire. Approximately 395 men, women, and children—almost all MacDonalds—suffocated and died.

Bearing these horrendous events in mind. Sam and I set out to find the hidden entrance of the cave. Less than three feet high and perhaps two feet wide, it was tucked in under an overhanging cliff, and was thus lost in the shadows. Without that snowfall, a rare event in this part of the Hebrides, the marauding MacLeods would never have found it either.

I removed my backpack, stuffed my flashlight into a jacket pocket, and proceeded to crawl on all fours into the entrance. Sam followed close behind. I was able to stand up after a distance of eight to ten feet. Switching on my light, I helped Sam exit from the tunnel and then pointed the beam to illuminate the interior.

The beam was lost in the vastness of the cavern that lay before us. Sam told me it stretched 230 feet ahead. The width of the cave spanned twenty feet, and the ceiling ranged a height of fifteen to thirty feet. Sam led me to the farthest recess of the cave, pointing out along the way where various groups of skeletons had been found. These must have been family groups that had huddled to die together.

At the back I turned off the flashlight. Standing quietly in the dark, I said a silent prayer as Sam informed me that most of the remains had not been removed for proper burial until the latter part of the last century.

It was a deeply moving, yet very disturbing, moment. It impressed upon me just how rough life had been for my Celtic ancestors of four hundred years ago. Those who managed to survive disease and privation still had to contend with the wrath of warring clans.

Isle of Rhum

RHUM "is controlled by the Nature Conservancy Council. Permission to visit the island during the holiday periods should be obtained well in advance from the Nature Conservancy, 12 Hope Terrace, Edinburgh.

"It is agreed that there should be no rescue liability falling on the island's scientific staff, and that climbers will comply with such guidance as may be given them from time to time about particular places within the mountain area which must be avoided for scientific reasons, or periods when the island has to be closed to visitors.

"Permission to stay on Rhum will be granted only to scientists, naturalists, and qualified mountaineers.

"Accommodation: there is none."

So reads the Scottish Mountaineering Club Guide, published in 1976.

I was, in a pub on the Isle of Skye. After reading this inhospitable treatise, I was more determined than ever to get to this island.

If I were in a large city, I would have asked a taxi driver for information on Rhum. But I was in the Hebrides, so I asked a 'publican,'—the man behind the bar.

"This guidebook that I have, published by the Scottish Mountaineering Club, says that Rhum is off-limits to visitors. Is that true?"

"Aye, it is," he said. "But you can go there. If you came all the way from Canada I don't think anyone will mind."

"Fine. How do I get there?"

"Take the mail boat. It stops once or twice a week. But don't tell them in the ticket office that you plan on going ashore."

"Where can I stay, since the book warns that there is no accommodation available?"

"Aye, that's what the book says. Would you like another pint of lager?"

"Sure."

"If you would like, I can telephone Mrs. MacIntosh."

"Why?"

"She lives on Rhum. Her husband works for the scientists there."

"Does she run a bed and breakfast?"

"No. But if I tell her you're from Canada—Nova Scotia especially—she'll give you accommodation. Great cook."

I left the publican a ten pound (twenty dollar) tip!

Rhum does not have a proper pier for docking a ferry, or mail boat. A small boat came out to meet us, as we wallowed in the ocean swells just beyond the entrance to Loch Scresort.

The Royal Mail was off–loaded, followed by several cartons of supplies, and then my knapsack. When I climbed down into the small craft, I timed my descent so that I was at the bottom of the ladder just as the boat rose to the wave's crest. Five years of summer employment on the Newfoundland coastal boats, during my university years,

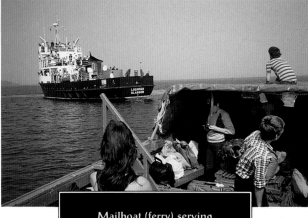

Mailboat (ferry) serving Rhum and the other islands (Eigg, Canna and Muck) that make up the Parish of the Small Isles.

Isle of Rhum. Twin peaks of Trollaval on the left.

taught me this technique. It's like riding a bicycle: once you learn how, you never forget.

Mrs. MacIntosh was waiting at the door when I arrived. Her home was a simple two–storey dwelling, made of stone and white in colour. Although sparsely furnished, my room on the second floor was nevertheless quite comfortable.

Rhum is a wonderful island, an island of extreme contrasts. Situated fifteen miles out from the mainland, it is four miles northwest of the Isle of Eigg and ten miles from the Isle of Skye. Shaped like a rough-cut diamond and only eight miles wide, it is the largest of the four islands that make up 'The Parish of the Small Isles.'

An island of towering mountains and long, lonely, glens, Rhum contains volcanic rocks of a type that is otherwise only found on the moon. Among its other treasures are a wildly extravagant castle and a mausoleum that was built in the form of a Greek temple. Sometimes called 'The

Forbidden Isle,' it is the site of the strongest gravitational pull in the British Isles.

For more than a century, Rhum was off-limits to all visitors and even today it has little to offer the conventional tourist. There are no pubs or restaurants, no shops or stores of any kind—in short, nothing to entertain or amuse visitors.

When I landed in Rhum in August of 1984 it had a population of twenty, fifteen of whom were employed by the Nature Conservancy Council and involved in ecological research of one kind or another. The exceptions were the school teacher and his wife, their two young students, and Mrs. MacIntosh.

In addition to being a paradise for geologists and mountain climbers, Rhum is a living laboratory where biologists, ecologists, and conservationists can observe animals such as red deer, wild goats, and Highland cattle, in an undisturbed and basically untouched environment.

However, it was not Rhum's laboratory that interested me. I was more intrigued by the fact that in 1826, during the height of the Highland Clearances, approximately 350 inhabitants of this island were evicted from their homes, herded on a boat, and shipped across the Atlantic Ocean to Nova Scotia. They were put ashore in a tiny community on the Strait of Canso called Ship's Harbour. Today we know it as Port Hawkesbury.

The adult passenger list included: 71 MacKenzies, 44 MacLeans, 37 MacKays, 20 MacMillans, 9 MacQuarries, 7 MacPhadens, 2 MacIssacs, 2 MacArthurs, 2 Stewarts, 1 Campbell, and 1 Cameron. The remaining passengers were children.

For centuries Rhum was owned by the Clan MacLean. Since half the island is mountainous, and the other half mostly bog and wetland, the island was never capable of supporting much of a population.

From the late Middle Ages down to the early nineteenth century, the population of this infertile island lived in desperate poverty. The people lived in appropriately named 'black houses,' which were simple stone dwellings with thatched roofs that were heated by peat fires. They desperately tried to grow enough potatoes and vegetables to feed their families, but the very nature of the terrain made this a very difficult task. Famine was a regular visitor to the island.

The abandoned graveyard in the ruined village of Kilmory contains a gravestone erected by Murdo Matheson in honour of his six children. Rebecca, seventeen, John, twelve, Christina Ann, eight, Murdo, six, William John, four, and Archie Duncan, seven months, all died within three days of each other, probably from a combination of famine and disease. We can assume that others met the same horrible fate.

Alexander MacLean, the owner of Rhum at the time of the Clearance, replaced his displaced people with an estimated eight thousand sheep. However, he soon realized that he did not have the manpower to properly care for these animals and his new venture was a dismal failure. Disease and malnutrition soon decimated his flocks.

In 1845, Alexander's son sold Rhum to an English country gentleman, the second Marquess of Salisbury. He stocked the hills with red deer and hatched a plan to turn the entire island into a private hunting estate. In 1857, his son initiated a second Clearance to Canada.

Over the next thirty years, the island changed ownership three times. In 1887 it was sold again, this time to a wealthy industrialist from Lancashire, England by the name of John Bullough.

When he died in 1891, the island passed to his son George, who immediately set out to make some fundamental changes. Just only twenty-two years old, and worth many millions, he literally had the world at his feet.

George fancied himself a Highland 'laird,' (lord) even though he was thoroughly English, and so he built a castle for himself.

This extravagant dwelling of red sandstone, shipped stone by stone from another island, was a perfect reflection of the ostentatious manner of its builder. He spared no expense in either its construction or its decoration.

Outfitted in kilts, workmen, were brought in from northern England. Soil for gardens and trees was shipped from the mainland. Greenhouses were built, so that he could offer his guests grapes and peaches. Small ponds stocked with salmon were linked by underground pipe to local streams, while another pond was stocked with imported turtles!

The building itself was filled with every modern convenience. Served by an internal exchange, rosewood and brass telephones, were strategically placed throughout the castle and in every bedroom. The guest bedrooms were outfitted with lavish baths and shower facilities, at a time when such things were unheard of even in Glasgow and Edinburgh.

A large and very ornate ballroom, with cut-glass chandeliers, hardwood floors, Oriental tapestries, and a musi-

Another view from the slopes of Trollaval, Isle of Rhum, with the Outer Hebrides on the horizon.

cians' gallery, was to provide the focal point for social gatherings that would attract famous and well-to-do guests from all over Britain, as well as the continent.

The piece de resistance, however, was the music room with its 'Orchestrium.' Manufactured in Germany this elaborate, mechanical organ was powered by an electric motor. Perforated rolls of paper, somewhat like those found in a player-piano, controlled an intricate system of valves that used air pressure to 'play' all the instruments of the orchestra, with the exception of the string section. Queen Victoria in London owned the only other Orchestrium of record.

The electricity that powered the Orchestrium and provided lighting for the castle was generated by hydroelectric power from a generator located in a small power house that had been built upstream from the castle. The power was delivered through underground cables, and the self-contained system was still functioning seventy years later.

Kinloch Castle was the most luxurious, and technologically advanced, residence in all of Scotland. When completed in 1901, at a cost of five hundred thousand dollars, more than one hundred people were employed to maintain the castle for the periodic visits of George and his family. Today it is worth several million.

Young George then proceeded to court, and eventually marry, a divorced noble woman from Paris. Building an extravagant castle, calling himself a 'laird,' and marriage to a divorced woman—all of this was too much for polite highland society. But then, the social elite of Scotland were never invited to his gatherings. The invited guests were usually from England or from the royal courts of Europe.

Kinloch Castle, Isle of Rhum.

Sir George (he was knighted in 1917) died in 1937, but his widow lived to the grand old age of ninety-eight. Lady Bullough sold the island to the Nature Conservancy Council in 1957 but she retained visitation rights for herself and her family.

On her death in 1967, Lady Bullough's body was returned to Rhum and interred in lonely Glen Harris, next to her husband. The family had chosen to build a mausoleum in this remote location, so that their parents could look out over the ocean towards England.

There is no temple to mark the site of the unknown Norse lady who was buried on top of the mountain known as 'Trollaval,' but then the Vikings were not famous for erecting temples. They much preferred to take temples, or anything else for that matter, apart.

Some say she was a Viking princess, but we don't know for sure. What we do know is that someone, presumably a young female, was buried on top of this mountain during the period of time that the Vikings controlled the Hebrides. That would make the grave well over a thousand years old.

On the morning that I set out to climb Trollaval (Mountain of the Trolls), Mrs. MacIntosh offered some local lore, and some advice. As she put together a packed lunch for me to take into the hills, she recounted the story of the grave and the cairn that are located on one of the two summits that crown Trollaval.

Situated approximately 2,300 feet above sea level, the cairn has increased in size over the centuries. Each individual who attempts to climb the mountain must carry a stone from sea level to the top, and add it to the cairn. Mrs. MacIntosh could not explain the rationale for this tradition.

She was also quite insistent that I be off the mountain before sundown. Again short on explanations, she made

The view from the slopes of Mount Trollaval, just before the 'dash' to the summit. The Outer Hebrides are visible on the horizon, over forty miles away.

me promise that I would do as I was told. After all, although she had never climbed to the top of any of the peaks on Rhum, this was her island and I should heed her word.

Shortly after eleven A.M., I donned my backpack and set off up Kinloch Glen. On reaching the top of a small ridge, I left the rough road behind and headed across the moor.

Skirting the shore of a small loch, I followed the flank of a lesser mountain until I reached the base of Trollaval. By this time the sun was high in the sky and the temperature had climbed into the high twenties (Celsius). This was very unusual for the Hebrides and, as a result, the climb was taking longer than expected.

After four hours I estimated that I was within five hundred feet of the summit. Removing my backpack, I sat on the end of a rocky ledge and lunched. Because of the heat, I had been going through water at a greater rate than

I had anticipated, and would soon have to turn to my reserve canteen.

The view from this height was overwhelming, and it increased my desire to reach the top. After a rest of thirty-minutes, I started my summit dash. Leaving my backpack on the ledge so that I could move faster, I set off with only my camera and my reserve water canteen. In less than half an hour I was on the first summit. The second, with its cairn, was less than fifty feet away.

The cairn was in front of me, right where Mrs. MacIntosh and the Scottish Mountaineering Guide Book had said it would be. It looked about thirty feet long and twenty feet high. I scrambled over to it and removed a small stone from my pocket. Tossing it on the cairn, I said a silent prayer, and returned to the first summit.

The view was extraordinary. Directly in front of me was the Isle of Eigg, with its famous An Sgurr and its ancient vit-

Isle of Rhum, Parish of the Small Isles, Inner Hebrides.

rified fort. Just one week before I had stood on its summit and looked across the four miles of water separating the two islands. Now I was standing on top of one of those peaks that had seemed as distant as the mountains of the moon.

Strung out behind Eigg, in a grand tableau that seemed to stretch from one end of the horizon to the other, were the countless peaks that made up the Highlands of mainland Scotland.

Off to my left, and ten miles away, lay the Isle of Skye, whose magnificent mountains I would explore in a later visit.

Off to my right, and forty miles away, were the Outer Hebrides. I could easily make out the islands of Harris and Lewis, as well as North and South Uist, Eriskay, Barra, and Barra Head.

All this was in addition to the other peaks that ranged around me, which were part of the mountain range known as the 'Cuillin of Rhum.' When viewed from the sea, from

the mail boat that carried me there, these same mountains had looked somewhat threatening—hazardous even. After all, their names are mainly Norse, and most had bore silent witness to untold horrors and atrocities down through the ages.

Yet here, atop Trollaval, all was peaceful and serene. It was now late in the afternoon, and very hot. I estimated that it would take me about two hours to make my descent, and I fully intended to be off the mountain before dark.

Mrs. MacIntosh's warning was not my main concern. From previous experience in even higher mountains, I knew to stay well within the limits of my capabilities. I was careful to avoid the highest cliff on Rhum, over one thousand feet tall, which was located on one of the flanks of Trollaval.

I lingered, reluctant to leave this special place and this special moment, sitting on a ledge and taking it all in.

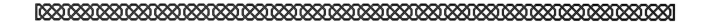

I was late getting off the mountain. The descent had not gone as easily as I had expected; the going was rough underfoot. I still had quite some distance to go when the sun dipped below the horizon and I had to break out a flashlight.

It took another forty minutes to reach the base of Trollaval. It was not a pleasant experience. I hate to admit it, but I felt that there was definitely something wrong with my being on the slopes of this mountain after sundown.

It was not the power of suggestion. It was something much more palpable than that. There was something unnatural about this place, and I knew it. I could feel it.

It wasn't that I saw anything, or heard anything. I didn't. In actual fact, it was what I didn't see, what I didn't hear, that was spooking me.

I felt a 'presence' of some sort, or maybe there were several. Not malevolent or evil, just intimidating, and alarming. I knew this was not something to trifle with, or to dismiss out of hand.

At no time did I fear for my personal safety. On the other hand, at no time did I have any desire, or interest, to linger. I was being strongly encouraged to vacate the lower slopes of this mountain as quickly as possible.

On reaching the road, I suddenly became aware of two headlights piercing the darkness, about one or two miles ahead. I knew right away what it was.

A search and rescue party that had been hastily assembled was setting out to look for me. I took off my backpack, took out a chocolate bar, and finished the remaining water in my reserve canteen.

Thirty minutes later I was sitting in Mrs. MacIntosh's kitchen. She had prepared a large lunch, including a hearty bowl of soup. Mr. MacIntosh poured me a second shot of Tallisker whisky, since the first 'drop of the hard stuff' had gone down pretty fast. I was not very hungry.

This wonderful, extremely hospitable couple, excused themselves and went to bed. As she left the kitchen, Mrs. MacIntosh looked at me, made the sign of the cross, and smiled.

When I retired for the night I found an open book on the small dresser next to my bed. It had not been there in the morning. Curious, I picked it up and looked at the cover. Harpoon at a Venture, by Gavin Maxwell. That told me nothing.

Picking it up, I began to read.

"Rhum is a strange place, eerie and haunted if ever a Hebridean island was. It is all mountain, hills as dark and savage as the Cuillins (Skye) themselves, and falling for the most part steeply to the sea. The hills even carry the name, the Cuillin of Rhum, but they seem to have a different soul, something older and more brooding. Their names are mainly Norse, given them long ago by the raiding longships...if there is a place where I could believe every Gaelic folk-tale and wild Celtic superstition, it is in their shadow."

It seems that I was not the first person to have had an unsettling experience in the hills of Rhum.

However, as I found out the next morning from Mrs. MacIntosh, I was one of the fortunate ones!

Loch Morar

I HAVE TRACED my genealogy back seven generations on my father's side. My paternal family tree looks like this:

1. Rannie
2. Ambrose (father)
3. Malcolm (grandfather)
4. Hughie (great-grandfather) Born in 1818, in Scotland. Three years old when he arrived in Nova Scotia, and five years old when he moved to Southwest Margaree.
5. Angus (great-great-grandfather) Came to Nova Scotia from Scotland in 1821, moved to Cape Breton in 1823, died in Upper Margaree in 1842.
6. Malcolm (great-great-great-grandfather) Never left Scotland.
7. Donald (great-great-great-great-grandfather).
8. Duncan (great-great-great-great-great-grandfather).

In spite of a great deal of searching, on both sides of the Atlantic, I have been unable to come up with authenticated birth dates for Angus, Malcolm, Donald, or Duncan.

I can, however, safely assume that Malcolm (number six) was probably alive during the Battle of Culloden Moor in 1746.

His father, Donald, was probably alive in 1700.

His grandfather, Duncan, lived in the 1600s and more than likely into the 1700s as well.

I can also assume that Angus and his family came to Nova Scotia in 1821 as a result of the Highland Clearances.

What I can state unequivocally, however, is precisely where in Scotland they lived.

Located on the mainland just across from the Isle of Skye is a starkly beautiful region of barren mountains and empty glens. Situated on a narrow neck of land between Loch Morar and the outer waters of the Sound of Sleat, Morar looks out across the sea to Skye, Rhum, and Eigg.

The focal point of the area is Loch Morar, whose waters harbour a legendary monster, much the same as the more famous one that is said to inhabit Loch Ness.

Scottish graffiti, Loch Morar.

Completely landlocked and more than twenty miles long, it is one of the largest lochs in Scotland. Over one thousand feet deep for most of its length, it is the deepest inland water in all of the British Isles.

Bonnie Prince Charles wandered among these hills after his defeat at Culloden, in 1746, and one of his followers, Lord Lovat, was captured on an island in the loch and later beheaded. This same island later became the site of a Roman Catholic College which became the official residence of the Pope's Vicar General of Scotland.

On my motorcycle I followed the secondary road that runs for a distance of several miles along the north shore of the loch. When the road came to an end I parked the bike and, hearing Gaelic–speaking voices, made my way up a short driveway and around behind a stone building. There I came face to face with Jimmy MacDonnell and Malcolm Arnold, who were fixing a farm tractor.

Loch Morar.

Malcolm was a school teacher who had come to Loch Morar 'on holiday' over twelve years ago. He had not missed a year since. Jimmy had lived here all his life, with the exception of the time he spent in the army during the Second World War.

During the war, Jimmy was a dispatch rider, who carried messages from one section of the front line to another. He travelled by motorcycle!

I was invited inside for a drink of whisky and then shown the path that would take me up into the mountains around the Loch. Jimmy also told me exactly where I could find some trace of the people who lived here before the time of the Clearances.

You can well imagine the feelings and emotion that came over me as I spent the next few hours wandering in these hills. In one of the empty glens I came across some ruins of small cottage-style buildings that I later found out dated back to the time of the Clearances.

As I sat down for lunch, the words of Peggy MacCormick, came to mind. Even in her old age, and many years after she and the rest of her family had been evicted from their ancestral home, Peggy would still shed tears at

Jimmy MacDonnell (standing)
and Malcolm Arnold, Loch Morar.

the mere thought of what had happened during that dreadful time. She died in 1894.

Peggy was a writer and those who remembered her stories often made mention of the fact that they had been much more moving in the original Gaelic. Although she lived on the Isle of South Uist in the Outer Hebrides, the scenes she witnessed as a young child, and later described so vividly, were repeated all over Scotland, including Morar.

"How we enjoyed ourselves in those far away days," she said. " Those were the happy days and there was neither sin nor sorrow in the world for us. But the Clearances came upon us, destroying all, turning our joy into misery, our gladness into bitterness, our blessing into blasphemy. Oh dear man, the tears come on my eyes when I think of all we suffered, and of the sorrows, hardships, and oppressions we came through."

This English translation can only suggest the sorrow and heartache of her simple words. In her case, the clan chief sold the islands of North and South Uist (Outer Hebrides) for less than $200,000 in today's money. The people, young and old, were herded to the shoreline like so many cattle and forced at gunpoint to board the waiting ship. Their simple, thatched cottages went up in smoke and their farm animals were confiscated.

She and her family, realizing what was about to happen, had taken to the hills a few days earlier. They survived several cold and wet nights without shelter before making their way by boat to a neighbouring island.

Loch Morar.

Another witness of the same eviction would later recall: "Were you to see the racing and chasing of policemen, you would think that you had been transported to the banks of the Gambia on the slave coast of Africa."

A few years after this eviction took place, the same islands were sold, this time for $400,000. (It seems that land speculation had become a new occupation for some of the former chiefs.)

As horrendous as the actual evictions were, they usually were followed by an even greater ordeal. All who left Scotland by ship, those 'cleared' as well as those who left of their own free will, had to endure unimaginable hardship.

From the very beginning the immigrants were the victims of con-men and sea captains. Typhus, cholera, and dysentery all took their toll. Those who reached the 'New World' considered themselves fortunate indeed.

In 1854 the London Times printed this first-hand account of just what it was like to take passage in an immigrant ship:

"The immigrant is shown a berth, a shelf of coarse pinewood in a noisome dungeon, airless and lightless, in which several hundred persons of both sexes and all ages are stowed away, on shelves stacked two feet apart. Each shelf is three feet wide and six feet long. Each immigrant believes that the shelf is his own and only finds when the anchor is up that he must share his space with a bedfellow.

"He finds that cleanliness is impossible. Among hundreds of men, women, and children, dressing and undressing, washing, quarrelling, fighting, cooking and drinking,

Cottage ruins from the time of the Highland
Clearances in the hills around Loch Morar.

one often hears the groans and screams of a fellow passenger in the last agonies of the plague (cholera)."

Stories such as these were foremost in my mind as I roamed through the hills of Loch Morar. At first I was angry that the government of the day made little or no attempt to prevent the Highland Clearances from taking place.

The evidence is quite clear that the government was a willing, and active, participant in the Clearances. In many cases the army and the local police force were used to ensure that serious resistance to the forced evictions did not develop.

The leaders of the Church, for the most part, stood by and raised no objections. They believed that the government was acting in the best interests of the population and that it would all work out for the best.

There is another important factor that must be taken into account with regard to the Clearances. The individuals who made up the highest levels of government, the Church, and the military, were from the upper classes of society. Typically, they had attended the same few elite schools and universities.

Thus there were vested interests at work whose first aim was the preservation of the existing social system. The obvious ill-treatment of large segments of society, given the fact that those affected were from the lower classes, was therefore not an issue of great concern in such a highly regimented and class-conscious society.

As I wandered in the hills, my initial feelings of shock were slowly tempered by the realization that as bad as the Clearances had been, there was a good side to them as well.

As rugged and starkly beautiful as the mountainous region around Loch Morar undoubtedly was, there was no escaping the fact that the land was barren and incapable of sustaining much in the way of agriculture. The same would hold true for dairy farming. There was no suitable area that could be used for pasture, let alone for the growing of hay or other grains.

It slowly dawned on me that my ancestors would surely have faced mass starvation, had they not been forced to leave. There was absolutely no way that these hills and glens could have supported the rapidly expanding population.

It started to mist as I made my way down from the hills. Just as I approached the motorcycle my solitude was shattered. The thunderous roar of powerful jet engines reverberated off the surrounding mountains as two Royal Air Force jet fighters flew up the loch at low level. I was rudely jolted back into the twentieth century.

As the aircraft receded in the distance, with the sound of their engines still echoing from the surrounding hills, one of them suddenly pulled up into a near vertical position. Rolling to the left, he reversed direction, and headed back towards me.

Rapidly approaching at a distance of no more than one hundred feet off the water, he tilted his aircraft slightly as he sped past, no more than three hundred feet away. His helmet was visible and I thought I could make out the wave of a hand. I stood there dumbstruck as he then pointed the nose of the aircraft skyward and surged into a near vertical climb.

My eyes followed him until he was no more than a speck in the distance, confident that he had probably been just as startled to see a large North American style touring motorcycle on the shores of Loch Morar as I had been to find my seclusion spoiled by the appearance of the two jets.

(In the days of the Cold War, Loch Morar was one of several large Scottish lochs that the Royal Air Force used for low-level flight training in mountainous terrain. With the end of the Cold War and the decline of communism, the flights have been discontinued.)

The Isle of Skye

VOICES. CAN'T BE! I was a bit startled. Who are they, and how did they get here?

I had just come down from the mountain known as 'Sgurr Na Stri' and, while on top, had a clear view of the only route to Loch Coruisk. I had followed it myself, earlier in the afternoon, as I wended my way in from the road at Kirkibost, by way of Camasunary.

It had been a solitary hike and, from my vantage point on high, I could tell that no one was following in my footsteps. So, where did these people come from?

I placed my knapsack on the ground and climbed to the top of a little ridge that would give me a view over the waters of Loch Scavaig. Sure enough, there they were. The chattering and frolicking of three adults and two children contrasted sharply with the solitude of the tranquil Loch.

Tied up to an iron pin which was embedded in a rock was a small boat about twenty feet long. They had obviously hired a local fisherman to take them over for a look at Loch Coruisk. I wondered if they had room for one more, on their return journey. If they did, it would sure as hell save me an arduous walk back.

The six–mile hike in to Loch Coruisk had taken almost four hours. The first three miles were relatively easy, with the first mile almost level. This was followed by an easy climb to the top of a col, a low saddle-shaped area between two mountains. On reaching that vantage point, I was rewarded with one of the finest panoramic

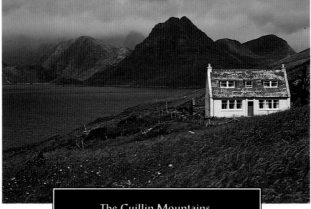

The Cuillin Mountains, from village of Elgol, Isle of Skye.

views in all of Scotland, the main ridge of the Cuillin Mountains on the Isle of Skye.

Dominating the north-south horizon, for a distance of seven miles, were twenty individual peaks. Of these, sixteen summits reached a height over three thousand feet! Known to mountaineers the world over, these peaks represent some of the most challenging climbs in Europe, outside the Alps.

I, however, had not come to Skye to climb in the Cuillin. That would be too foolhardy, especially alone. It was one thing to go into the mountains of Mull, Rhum, and other islands, on my own, because those journeys were basically long walks. Just put one foot in front of the other, and start making your way uphill— that was all.

I was frequently struck by the number of people who went 'into the hills' in Ireland and Scotland. Because of the nature of the landscape, and the almost total absence of forest cover, it was not uncommon to find entire families out hill walking. You could park your car almost anywhere, put on your hiking boots, and head for the hills.

The Scottish Mountaineering Society even divided the sport into four categories:

Walking, which is no fancier than the word implies;

Rambling, which refers to simple climbs over small hills and dales. A bit more effort but no danger;

Scrambling, which involves using your hands from time to time to help navigate over steep or broken terrain. This could be dangerous, especially without the proper

Hiking path to Loch Coruisk, Isle of Skye.

footwear and protective clothing.

Climbing, which is serious business! This form of mountaineering calls for formal climbing equipment such as ropes, harness, and rock axes. Even with the proper equipment, it's very dangerous.

Descending from the saddle to the beach at Camasunary was easy. From here on, however, the going got tough. The path wound its way around the base of a large mountain, and much of its three-mile length required a fair bit of scrambling. There were also boggy patches and areas that were wet enough to avoid.

Just when I thought the worst of it was over, I came upon the infamous 'Bad Step.' A thirty-foot section of near vertical rock diagonally cut by a wide crack, it is the most serious obstacle on the route to Loch Coruisk.

To cross it requires a good head for heights, as well as confidence in one's 'scrambling' ability. Natural hand-holds in the rock made it relatively easy to place my feet, one after the other, in the wide fault that nature had provided. If I had lost my footing, I only faced a twenty-five to thirty foot drop into the water.

The Bad Step was once at the heart of considerable turmoil in Scottish climbing circles. In 1968, the British Army announced its intention to use explosives to blast a path

Cuillin Mountains, Isle of Skye.

across the 'Bad Step,' in order to make it easier for tourists to visit Loch Coruisk.

There was a great public outcry, as if the destruction of an ancient monument had been announced. The fact that the British Army was behind it, and that plans had been put in place without any consultation with the Scottish authorities, only added fuel to the flame.

The turmoil reached as far as the floor of the House of Commons in London. Fortunately, common sense came into play, and the plan was scrapped. The Bad Step, on the footpath to Loch Coruisk, would remain inviolate. A national heirloom, the Loch itself would remain untouched and undisturbed by hordes of visitors.

A sheet of water two miles long, Loch Coruisk lies among glacier-polished rock slabs at the foot of the Cuillin. It has provided the inspiration for many of Scotland's greatest artists and writers. Surrounded by three thousand foot peaks, its location and splendid isolation have led many to regard it the most striking combination of mountain and loch scenery in all of Scotland.

After spending three hours exploring in the vicinity of the loch, including the scramble to the peak of Sgurr Na Stri, I was beginning to dread the six-mile return hike to my car. That's why Skipper Angus MacLean and his day-party were such a welcome sight.

Loch Coruisk, Isle of Skye.

He graciously offered to take me back with them, to the tiny fishing village of Elgol. For their part, the other passengers, a Stewart family from Edinburgh, offered to give me a lift to my car, which I had parked about six miles away.

The view from the boat, as we made our way from Loch Coruisk to Elgol, was extraordinary. The Scottish Mountaineering Guide brags that this view is not only the most striking combination of mountain and sea in the British Isles, it is the most outstanding such view in the world!

The Gaelic description of Skye is "Eilean A' Cheo fo sgail nam beannmor" ("The Isle of Mist under the shadow of great mountains"). Many consider it to be the loveliest of all the Hebrides. Sixty miles long, it is almost impossible to state its width with any accuracy, because of the indented nature of its two thousand mile coast.

The sea governs all aspects of life on Skye. No part of it is more than five miles from the ocean, and as many as fifteen major bays indent the shoreline. The sea is visible from every hilltop and the climate of Skye, as well as that of every island in the Inner and Outer Hebrides, is moderated by the warm waters of the Gulf Stream.

Since there are no railways or airports, all visitors must cross over the sea to Skye. For the first–time visitor, the voyage is always a bit of an adventure, whether the Cuillin mountains are drenched in mist and rain, or shimmering in a summer heat wave.

The Quirang, Isle of Skye.

Most of the islanders still make their living from crofting (tending a small plot of land near their house) and fishing, and the old Celtic traditions remain well intact. Celtic myth and legend abound, and the island has close ties with Bonnie Prince Charlie and the revolt of 1745.

The present population of Skye is around eight thousand. An early census in 1755 showed a population of just over eleven thousand; by 1841 it had more than doubled to twenty-three thousand. Large-scale emigration ensued later in Skye than in most of the other islands in the Hebrides, but when it did come, it was devastating.

In 1846 and 1847, a catastrophic potato famine struck Skye, the same disease that brought privation and hunger to Ireland. By 1849 over five thousand people were on 'relief.' The government cared for them, but they were expected to work in exchange for food. Eight hours of work earned two pounds of meat, with an extra half pound for every child, and three quarters of a pound for your wife! By this time, the Highland Clearances were now well under way on the island. It has been estimated that in the forty years between 1835 and 1875, approximately 7,000 families were evicted from their lands. If we figure on an average of five people per family, this represents about 35,000 men, women, and children.

Events finally came to a head in 1882 with the Battle of the Braes. This spontaneous uprising took place when some crofting families refused to obey their eviction notices. In spite of dire threats, they refused to leave their ancestral homes in this peaceful and fertile region of central Skye.

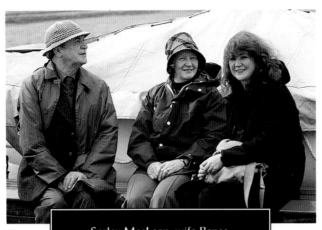

Sorley MacLean, wife Renee, and daughter , on ferry from Isle of Skye to Isle of Raasay.

According to Sorley MacLean, Scotland's greatest living Gaelic poet, the affair was to have far-reaching consequences, far greater that anyone could have imagined at the time. In fact, this skirmish would later become known as the 'Last Battle Fought On British Soil.'

Sorley knows a lot about 'The Braes.' He should, since he has come to know this region intimately ever since he was old enough to walk.

For Sorley was born and raised on the small island of Raasay, located just a short ten-minute ferry ride from Skye.

From his earliest days, Sorley could look across the Sound of Raasay to Skye and see the fertile strip of land along the shore known as The Braes. Many years later, after Sorley's poetry had come well known, he chose to make his home there.

I first met Sorley and his wife Renee in 1979, when they were guests of honour at an international gathering of Celtic writers held in Baddeck, Nova Scotia. This was one of many Celtic cultural events that took place as part of the first International Gathering Of The Clans that was held in North America. That it took place in Nova Scotia was fitting, indeed.

As it turned out, Sorley was a very close personal friend of Major MacLeod, my former Celtic studies teacher at St. Francis Xavier University. He was also a close friend of my granduncle, Monsignor P.J. Nicholson, who was a noted Celtic scholar in his own right.

When I visited Sorley in The Braes during my 1980 tour, he showed me the approximate site where the local police had tried to enforce the eviction order on the Clan Chief. Several young men who had been arrested a few days earlier resisted, and they were sent off to jail on the mainland. The nature of the arrests, and the manner in which they had been carried out, were hardly to the liking of the peaceful residents of this gentle island. Crowds of angry young men and women, as well as aging veterans, rushed to the crofters' defense.

There were many veterans on Skye, for the island had a long history of sending young men to serve with the Highland regiments of the British Army. For most of them, it was a chance to escape the poverty and despair that went with the crofting lifestyle, and it was also a chance to see the world. They had fought valiantly for 'king and country' in most of Britain's colonial wars, and in the farthest reaches of the Empire.

Those fortunate enough to survive were rewarded with quite substantial military pensions, and they returned to Skye to live out their retirement years. A goodly number of them settled in the area surrounding The Braes, as it was not too far from the island's only town. In fact, the service pensions that these men received played a major role in the economy of the island in the latter half of the nineteenth century.

When the police returned a few days after the arrests, with reinforcements, the residents were ready and waiting. They roughed up the constables and seized their weapons, contrary to their reputation as peaceful folk who were slow to anger and hard to rile.

The author, hiking in the Quirang, Isle of Skye.

Immediately the British dispatched a Royal Navy warship to the waters around The Braes, with a detachment of Royal Marines on board. Fifty armed police and militia were also sent over from Glasgow, but the crofters refused to budge.

When the Royal Marines came ashore, they confronted a motley contingent of senior citizens, irate young men and women, and enraged veterans of His Majesty's Army. The Marine's respect for the veterans prevented their advance, and a tense stand–off ensued. The revolt of 'the Crofters Army,' as it came to be called in the press, became front page news in Glasgow, Edinburgh, and most important of all, in London.

Cooler heads would eventually prevail. The Royal Marines, the police, and the militia were all withdrawn, and the crofters were told, on direct orders from London, that they could remain on their land. Most important of all, the British government realized that the times were indeed changing, and that it had become necessary to investigate the whole problem of land ownership in Scotland. A Royal Commission was struck to look into the matter.

In December, 1883, the release of the commission's report brought widespread outrage, as the British public became aware of the cruel and sadistic methods that had been employed, in the name of the Crown, to bring about

Part of the mountain range known
as the 'Black Cuillin,' Isle of Skye.

the eviction of innocent people. There was a great outpouring of sympathy for the crofters.

The passing of the Crofters' Holding Act in 1886 effectively brought about the end of the Highland Clearances. From then on, even though they still did not own the land, the crofters were protected by the full force of British law.

They could not be evicted, for any reason, and their croft, or plot of land, would pass from generation to generation. Any reasonable increase in rent would have to be negotiated between the owner of the croft and a special commission that was set up to ensure that the rulings of the Royal Commission were enforced.

For the first time in hundreds of years, the tenant farmers of Scotland could feel secure.

In 1955, a new and revised Crofters' Act was passed by Parliament. This was followed in 1965 by the formation of The Highlands and Islands Development Board, whose mandate was to promote the economic well being and development of the Highlands and the Hebrides.

The Highlands and Islands, the most chronically depressed region in all the British Isles, had finally come into the twentieth century.

The Dingle Peninsula

HULLO! HULLO! Anybody home?"

Since there was no reply, I proceeded down the small hallway and took the first door on the left. I found myself in the empty lounge of the Granville Hotel, facing a battered upright piano that had obviously been the site of several late-night musical events. The far wall sported a large fireplace while, in the corner to my right, mahogany and oak accented the small, yet cosy, bar.

I continued on down the hall, made a left turn, and came to a set of stairs.

"Hullo! Hullo!"

The reply from upstairs was soft and gentle, with a musical lilt to the voice that you only find in this part of western Ireland.

"Can I help you?"

"I'd like to know if I can get a room. Do you have one available?"

"I'll go and get Billy. I'll just be a minute."

Rather than wait at the foot of the stairs I made my way back to the lounge and sat down at the piano. I was well into my second tune by Scott Joplin when the young lady with the lyrical lilt in her voice returned, accompanied by the manager.

I finished, with a flourish, and stood to meet them both.

"Billy Granville," said a tall man. "Stephanie here tells me you need a room."

"That's right. For a few days, if possible."

"Bed and breakfast?"

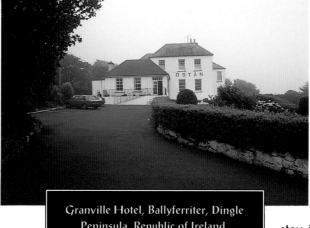

Granville Hotel, Ballyferriter, Dingle Peninsula, Republic of Ireland.

"Have you got one with a shower? I plan to do some hill-walking."

"Yes. We have a vacancy, with shower, but I'll have to get Stephanie to make it up. We weren't expecting any further guests. Breakfast is from 7:30 to 9:00."

"I guess I'll miss it; I like to sleep late."

"In that case, breakfast will be from nine to ten-thirty, or even later, depending on when you rise."

"Thanks, but that won't be necessary. I seldom eat breakfast."

"In that case, Stephanie will pack you a lunch you can take into the hills."

By this time, my host was smiling broadly. I replied, "I think I'm going to like it here, Billy."

"Have you been driving for some time?"

"Yes, I came down from Valentia Island expecting to stay in Dingle, but the town was booked up. Then I got lost on these back roads. The Gaelic signs threw me for a loop."

"Good God, man, you drove down from Valentia. That's almost a hundred miles!"

"Not very far in Canadian terms; mind you our roads are a hell of a lot better."

"Care for a pint?"

With that, Stephanie went off to make up my room at the top of the stairs while Billy escorted me back to the lounge. I ordered up a pint of Smithwicks (Smith-icks) dark

An interesting combination of old and new religion.
Prehistoric Celtic Standing Stone with religious carvings,
and spire of nineteenth century Catholic Church.
County Donegal, Republic of Ireland.

ale, which Billy produced from an ornate tap behind the bar.

We were soon joined by a lawyer from Cork, a fine gentleman who asked some very pointed questions about the state of the Canadian economy and the role of the Province of Quebec in Confederation. We had an animated, three-way conversation, while Billy made sure that I was supplied with Smithwicks, and that he and his legal friend had enough whiskey.

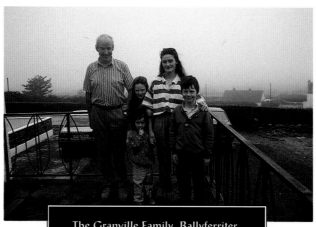

The Granville Family, Ballyferriter, Dingle Peninsula, Republic of Ireland.

I later found out that this lawyer made a point of returning each year to this family-run hotel, whenever he was 'on holiday.' He had stumbled on Granville's, quite by accident, more than twelve years ago, and kept coming back.

Like the lawyer from Cork, I too, came upon the place quite by accident. On entering the Dingle Peninsula, my original intention had been to find a place to stay in the Town of Dingle. But it was the second last week in August, and the town was full of tourists, mainly from Germany, Italy, and Holland.

After making a few inquiries I was advised to travel a few miles outside of town where I should have no problem finding a bed and breakfast accommodation.

Instead, I got lost. I spent the better part of an hour driving the back roads of the Dingle Peninsula. The fact that most of these roads were signposted in Irish Gaelic only added to my general confusion, especially when I came to a three or four-way junction!

It was in this manner that I finally found myself in the tiny village of Ballyferriter: a church, a post office, a police station, two hotels, and several pubs. (Only a few miles away was the village of Castlegregory with a population of 190; it boasted six pubs!)

Situated in an area of immense historical interest, and surrounded by scenic beauty, Ballyferrier turned out to be an excellent place to use as a touring centre. And Billy turned out to be an excellent guide.

The Dingle is one of three picturesque peninsulas that jut out into the Atlantic Ocean from County Kerry, in western Ireland. The entire peninsula has superb mountain and coastal scenery and there is no shortage of prehistoric and early Christian/Celtic monuments.

The Dingle Peninsula is also one of the 'pure' Gaelic–speaking areas still found in the west of Ireland. A centre for authentic Celtic music and Gaelic singing, its remote location and narrow roads have helped ensure that the vast majority of tourists would pass it by.

(Billy later explained that the Town of Dingle had recently achieved a bit of a reputation in certain European countries as a result of a television documentary. Fortunately, this interest did not extend to the rest of the peninsula!)

The next morning I was up bright and early at 11:20 A.M. and off into the mountains. Sarah had kindly left a packed lunch on the floor, just outside my room, and Billy had enclosed some written suggestions on easy routes to the top.

Surrounded on three sides by the Atlantic Ocean, the narrow Dingle Peninsula is one of the finest regions in all of Ireland to explore on foot. Towering cliffs, rugged mountains, low coastal valleys, and gorgeous beaches, ganged up on my senses and left an indelible imprint.

As if the contemplation of stunning scenery were not enough, there is also the quite extraordinary concentration of superb archaeological and historical sites, many of which are hidden away in the most unusual nooks and crannies,

Seventh century Gallarus Oratory, Dingle Peninsula, Republic of Ireland. The finest surviving example of an early Christian Oratory (Church). Built of horizontal layers of stone, without the use of mortar or cement, the building is still watertight after thirteen centuries.

and therefore only accessible to those who travel on foot.

These artifacts from our distant past are not comparable to such monumental structures as those of Stonehenge, in England, or Newgrange, on the outskirts of Dublin. Rather, a good part of their beauty and charm lies in the modest nature of their construction, and in the realization that they were built by ordinary people, for quite ordinary reasons.

Located at the extreme western edge of Europe, the peninsula's strategic position meant that it served as a repository for knowledge and culture, especially during the Dark Ages. In archaeological terms, its relative isolation and lack of economic development meant that virtually all of its archaeological sites remain intact.

Although Ireland had been inhabited ever since the retreat of the last ice age, it was only after 9000 B.C. that stone age man arrived in any numbers. Over the next three thousand years, small groups roamed the coasts, hunting, fishing, and collecting whatever food was available. Much of the country was covered in dense forests, which made penetration of the interior very difficult.

The Neolithic, or late Stone Age, arrived in Ireland sometime between 5000 and 4000 B.C., and brought about the development of agriculture and an increase in population. This period in time was also known as the Megalithic (Big Stone) Age because it was during this peri-

'The Sleeping Irish Giant.' When viewed from a certain angle, Great Blasket Island, Dingle Peninsula, shows the reclining form of a giant. From the right: forehead, nose, jaw, hands folded on his lap, knees, and feet.

od that the 'standing stones' were erected and the many Neolithic tombs were built.

Since no defensive structures dating from this time have ever been found, we can assume that the people lived a relatively peaceful existence, cultivating the soil, domesticating animals, and slowly pushing back the frontiers of the primeval forest.

It was also during Neolithic times that southwest Ireland, and the Dingle Peninsula in particular, became an important part of a major trade route that ran from North Africa and the Mediterranean Sea to the fjords of Scandinavia.

Sailing the ocean, but always staying within sight of land, these early navigators stopped in Spain, Portugal, the western parts of France, England, Scotland, and Ireland. A substantial export trade developed between these regions as well as a vigorous intellectual exchange. Ideas and customs flowed back and forth between these areas as easily as did the trade in metals and gold.

As a result of all this, the Dingle Peninsula was perhaps the first part of ancient Ireland to enjoy the fruits of early civilization.

By the time Ireland entered the Iron Age (c.800 B.C. to 400 A.D.), the Celts had arrived from the continent of Europe and Ireland was about to enter its Golden Age.

The Celts completely dominated the previous inhabitants of Ireland and were to exert an influence that continues to exist, even down to the present day.

Beach at Slea Head, Dingle Peninsula, used in the making of the movie 'Ryan's Daughter.' An entire Irish village was reconstructed in the hills above Slea Head for the filming of this movie.

With the arrival of Christianity, about 400 A.D., the Dingle Peninsula became one of the major centres of religious growth in Ireland. More than fifty sites of early Christian settlements have been identified, most at the western end of the peninsula.

I spent the next four days hill-walking and exploring. Each morning my packed lunch was waiting, just outside the door, along with hiking instructions and other helpful notes.

The long cool evenings were spent in conversation with Billy and his enchanting guests. Stephanie introduced me to her friend Sarah, who was also a college student. An accomplished pianist in her own right, Sarah and I spent part of each evening playing duets on the battered instrument.

On the Monday before I was to leave, I drove into the town of Dingle to look around, since a steady rain had put an end to my planned hill-walking. Billy suggested that since I was interested in traditional Irish music, I should check out a little pub called 'An Dorus Beag' (The Little Door). Although Monday night was usually a slow night, as it is in most towns on both sides of the Atlantic, he figured there just might be some activity there.

Billy was right. There are fifty-two pubs in Dingle town, (which boasts a year–round population of just 1,500) and on that particular Monday night only one of them was offering live music: An Dorus Beag.

But the music had not been planned, or advertised. It just happened. It seems that four young musicians from

Modern shipwreck of coastal freighter on the rocks of Slea Head, Dingle Peninsula.

Galway were in town, on holiday. They had made some inquiries with their instruments under their arms, and all fingers pointed to An Dorus Beag.

When I entered the small pub shortly after seven in the evening, the quartet from Galway was already playing. They seemed unconcerned that there was no one else in the place, except the bartender. They were not playing for an audience; they were playing for themselves.

I armed myself with a pint of Smithwicks and took a seat over by the large fireplace. Directly in front of me, the four from Galway sat on a wooden bench that ran underneath the window. From the dishes on the table in front of them, it was clear that they had just finished eating, and that music was to be the dessert.

And what music! A selection of traditional Irish slip-jigs was immediately followed by two Irish reels from County Kerry. They shyly acknowledged my applause and, after a short pause for refreshment, set to work again: two fiddles, a tin whistle, and a bodhran (hand–held drum). The low ceiling, made from hand–hewn wooden beams, provided excellent acoustics, which only served to enhance the quality of the music.

I was fascinated with the fiddle playing of the young woman who seemed to be the natural leader of the group. Maureen Fahy, from Ballinasloe, County Galway, was clearly not your average folk fiddler.

Spontaneous 'pub session,' Ballyferriter, Dingle Peninsula, Republic of Ireland.

Although she obviously had immense natural talent, it was evident that she had received some expert instruction from one or more fiddlers (violinists) who had some knowledge of Classical violin technique.

Whereas most traditional fiddle players only make use of the upper part of the violin bow, she used the full length. This gave her playing a sonority and resonance that is often lacking in folk music.

While most traditional fiddle players keep their left hand bent up under the finger board, in a horizontal manner, she held her hand in a near vertical position. She supported the finger board with only her thumb and the inner part of her index finger. This gave her much greater flexibility, freedom of movement, and greater speed.

She also possessed a very flexible wrist, another characteristic of someone with professional training. Most traditional fiddlers use their arm to control the movement of the bow. Her arm was almost stationary.

Within an hour, several other people ventured into the pub. From their rapport with the bartender it was obvious that they were 'regulars.' The word had gone out among the music community that a 'sessiun' was under way at An Dorus Beag.

('Sessiun' is Irish Gaelic for a spontaneous musical event. Brought to America, the term was taken up by jazz musicians, who coined the term 'jam session.' 'Sessiun' would be equivalent to 'Ceilidh' in Scotch Gaelic.)

A bearded young man with a guitar was the first local musician to join the group. I later found out that he hailed from Australia. He had arrived in Dingle two years before, and never left. That he was an extremely accomplished guitarist was evidenced by his ability to pick out the often intricate patterns of notes that were required in order to keep up with the likes of Maureen Fahy.

By the time the bartender signalled 'last call' at 10:30, the three small rooms that made up the pub were packed. There was not a German, Dutch, or Italian tourist in the place. They were all locals, and all traditional music lovers.

When the lights were turned on, I counted eleven musicians sitting in front of me: three violins; two accordions; two flutes; two guitars; one tin whistle; and one bodhran! I have never experienced such a spontaneous outpouring of music in any of my travels.

Maureen invited me to follow them to a house party a short distance away. Reluctantly, I had to decline. Not only did I have to leave early in the morning, I still had to navigate my way back to Ballyferriter, a distance of twelve miles.

Arriving just before midnight, miraculously without getting lost, I found the front door unlocked and a light still on in the lounge. I entered the room to switch the light off and, there, on a table under the lamp, was a tray with a chicken sandwich and a handful of cookies. Next to the tray, Billy had left a pint of Smithwicks.

The Cheshire Lads

SO IT'S CANADA you're from then. We don't get many Canadians in Derry. In fact we don't see many tourists at all these days, ever since the 'Troubles' started."

Shaun O'Leary had the ruddy complexion and jovial manner of one who had spent a lifetime behind a bar, making others feel at ease and welcoming strangers with a ready smile and a cold pint."

Like the vast majority of pubs in Ireland, his was a home as well as a place of business. In the family kitchen, his wife had prepared the meal that I had just washed down with two pints of dark, Irish ale. Even though it was after normal meal hours, traditional Irish hospitality had seen to it that I was properly fed.

Howie Allen and I had just checked in at a bed and breakfast down the street. It was very well kept, and only about $14.00 each, Canadian. This was Howie's first trip to Northern Ireland and he was hesitant to go out after dark. He opted to stay behind and write a few post cards, saying he would join me later.

We had been in Derry less than an hour, yet we had already received a briefing from our boarding lady on the stark reality of daily life in this part of a divided Ireland. This city of approximately fifty thousand souls has been riddled with strife and trouble for the last several hundred years. And today, when terrorism hits Northern Ireland, it usually hits hardest in Derry.

Derry (the British name 'Londonderry' is not popular) is a city divided, both along religious and ethnic lines. Like the rest of this troubled nation, Derry has long been split by conflict between pro-British Protestants and anti-British Catholics. It is a conflict that to date has defied all rational attempts to seek a solution.

"The 'Troubles, lad," explained the publican. "That's what we call it. Over three thousand dead. The British Army came here in 1969, to calm things down. They're still here. The killing still goes on.

"Last January, David McRae was killed outside his girlfriend's home in Bogside (a Catholic suburb), simply because he was Protestant and she was Catholic.

"In May, John Davey, a Protestant pipe-fitter on his way to work, was shot by two men when he stopped at a traffic signal. He was shot by Protestant gunmen who thought he was a police informer. They shot the wrong man!"

We had stepped into this 'other' world earlier that afternoon when, travelling on motorcycles, we approached a border crossing just west of Derry. It was a British military checkpoint, complete with machine guns and sand bags.

One of the flak-jacketed soldiers who examined our passports pointed at the olive green military-issue sweater I was wearing, and asked: "Are you in the Canadian Army!"

When I replied that I was not, and that I had purchased the sweater in a war-surplus outlet, he said: "I

Heavily armed police stopping traffic at border crossing with Northern Ireland.

Even after we were cleared at the roadblock outside of Belfast, the soldiers remained vigilant. They could joke and carry on, but they could never relax.

wouldn't wear that sweater around here, mate. You might end up with a bullet in your back! You look like a British officer, and a pretty stupid one at that."

I lost no time replacing the sweater with a leather jacket.

The next morning we were up early and on our way. It was seventy miles to Belfast and twenty more to the port of Larne. From there it was a two-hour ferry crossing to Scotland. This was why we ended up in Northern Ireland; it saved a long journey across the Irish Republic, the Irish Sea, Wales, and Northern England.

We were making good time on our motorcycles when, only ten miles from Belfast, we rounded a turn and came face to face with the British Army.

Both sides of the highway were sealed off. An armoured vehicle sat in the middle of the road, while on either side a soldier lay prone behind a machine gun. We braked to a hard stop and encountered several heavily armed men.

I was in the lead and they told me to get off the bike. When Howie began to do the same he was immediately told, at gun point, to stay put. I was escorted from the road into a small clearing where I stood in front of a superior officer. I was told to produce documents, which I did. Passport; driver's licence; credit cards; airline tickets; and even my Nova Scotia Teacher's Union card.

While all this was going on, at gunpoint, a corporal off to one side was flipping through a file folder of small I.D. type photographs. He was obviously checking for my photo. They also asked me to provide a sample of my handwriting, which they then compared with the signature on my documents.

Street scene, Catholic suburb, Belfast, Northern Ireland.

There was, however, a hitch. We were Canadians, driving German motorcycles with British licence plates, which we had rented in London. My papers were in order, with one exception. I had no 'Green Card,' an international insurance card that is mandatory for all rentals in the British Isles and Europe.

I tried to explain that our cards were not ready when we picked up the motorcycles in London. Rather than waste valuable time, I gave the rental company a friend's address in Scotland, and asked them to send the cards once they arrived.

When asked to produce further identification, I replied that I had none. But, I did add that my friend Howie had a rather special form of I.D.

With that we returned to the highway and approached Howie, who was still sitting on his motorcy-

cle, at gunpoint. He produced from his wallet a card indicating that he was a Major in the Canadian Militia, the Second Battalion Nova Scotia Highlanders (Cape Breton), to be exact.

Howie then proceeded to answer a number of pointed questions that required an insight into the military that could only be known to a person who had close ties to the services. Finally, one question broke the tension.

"What's the name of the British regiment that the Nova Scotia Highlanders are twinned with?"

"The Cheshire Regiment," was Howie's reply.

With that the interrogating officer broke into a wide grin, shook hands with Howie and then myself, and he replied: "We're Cheshire lads. I've been in Nova Scotia. You put on a great Tattoo in Halifax."

BOBBY SANDS M
JOE McDONNELL

FRANCIS HUGHES

KEVIN LYNCH

KIERAN DOHERTY TD

IN HONOUR

RAY McCREE

MARTIN HURSO

PATSY O'HA

TOM McELWE

MICHAEL DEVI

This wall in Belfast honours Irish 'Hunger Strikers'
who starved themselves to death.

(The Twenty-Second Cheshire Regiment, over three hundred years old, won their first battle honours with General Wolfe at the first Siege of Louisbourg. Thus the connection with the Cape Breton battalion.)

We spent the next hour with the Cheshire lads. Even when talking and joking, one of their number was constantly watching the surrounding countryside, while others continued to stop and search traffic.

They had lost one of their 'mates' a few days earlier, to a car bomb. Several others had been seriously injured. The next day was July twelfth, William of Orange Day, one of the most important religious holidays of the year. It was a 'holy day' that usually brought out the worst in both sides of the religious conflict.

As we made ready to leave, Howie put a question to the young soldier who had held him at gunpoint on his motorcycle.

"Why wouldn't you let me get off the bike!"

"As long as you were on the bike, mate, I knew those saddlebags wouldn't explode!"

The Cheshires were not taking any chances.

❖   ❖   ❖

THE KINTYRE PENINSULA, Scotland's longest, stretches for fifty miles from the famous Mull (point) of Kintyre in the south to the shores of Loch Fyne and the village of Lochgilphead in the north. From the famous lighthouse at the Mull of Kintyre you can easily make out the outline of Northern Ireland, only eleven miles away.

Exactly ten years after my encounter with the Cheshire regiment, I left Lochgilphead and pointed my rental car south. I had three hours to make the terminal at Kennacraig, for the ferry to the Isle of Islay was due to leave at 6:20 P.M.

The owner of a petrol (gas) station had suggested that if I wanted to see some very rugged and isolated country I should take a little–used secondary road along the west side of the Kintyre peninsula. I would have panoramic views of several of the Inner Hebrides and would rejoin the main road not too far from the ferry terminal.

The fellow did caution me that it was a 'slow road,' I could not expect to drive very fast, there might be animals on the road, and I might even find parts of the road off-limits.

As it turned out, I had to drive most of it in second gear. To call it a road was a bit of an exaggeration, for it consisted of two tracks with a ridge of grass running down the center.

Passing places were located every now and again, but the virtual absence of traffic made it unnecessary for me to use them. There seemed to be very little in the way of homes or people, just mile after mile of gorgeous scenery and flocks of sheep roaming the mountains.

Finally, after about eight or nine miles, I came upon my first oncoming car; a beautiful silver–coloured Jaguar, the XJE version. We both came to a halt as soon as we caught sight of each other and, since he was closer to a passing spot than I was, he obligingly backed up and pulled off the road.

As I approached in first gear, he rolled down his window and I pulled up alongside to have a chat. On this type of Scottish back road you often had a 'good chat' with the drivers of oncoming vehicles. It was a good opportunity to find out just what sort of road conditions lay ahead.

To my surprise I was greeted not by a thick Scottish accent but rather by the suave tones of a British gentleman, of obviously high breeding and, to judge by the pristine condition of his vehicle, quite wealthy as well.

"Good afternoon," he said. "Rather wonderful day for a drive, although I must say that there is a bit of bother ahead. Not much, really, but the lads are about and you know what that means, especially in August!"

"Well, I'm from Canada, over here on vacation. What exactly do you mean by a 'bit of bother'?"

"From Canada, you say! Jolly good! Must be a smashing experience for a Canadian to drive on these roads. Just down there, about a mile or so, you'll run into them. Don't let them startle you. After they ask a few questions, you'll be on your way."

He was friendly enough, but didn't have the time for a lengthy chat.

"Well I must be off," he said. "I have to make Glasgow, tonight. Board meeting in the morning. Right you are, enjoy your holiday!"

A little more than a mile later I slowly surmounted the crest of a steep hill and came upon a stunning scene. There in front of me, across a narrow stretch of water, lay the Isle of Jura, with its famous mountains called "The Paps" starkly outlined against the late afternoon sun.

Off to the right, staring at me from behind a wire fence, were six or seven of the most attractive, long–haired, Highland cattle that I had ever seen.

Off to my left, no more than half a mile away, was the magnificent outline of the Royal yacht, Britannia, with three flags flying from her masts.

Right in front were the 'lads.' There were three military men, all armed, and no smiles!

"What were these soldiers doing, on this minor back road in the Kintyre Peninsula?" I wondered. As I quickly braked to a halt, it all fell into place.

My recent conversation with the British driver that I had just passed about one mile back. His comment that "there was a bit of bother just ahead" and his reference to the "lads." Then the sudden appearance of the Royal yacht, Britannia!

Royal Yacht Britannia with Highland cattle.
Kintyre Peninsula, Scotland.

"Step out of your vehicle, please?" He was dead serious, as were the other two who stationed themselves on either side of the car. His sub-machine gun was slung on his shoulder but his two 'mates' were pointing their weapons directly at me. I gingerly stepped out of my vehicle.

"Identification!"

"It's in my jacket, on the back seat."

He motioned me to move away from the vehicle while he reached through the open window and removed my jacket. He checked it out with the palms of his hands and then passed it to me.

"American?"

"Canadian."

With this he gave a hint of a smile and asked me to produce my passport. I did. He looked it over very carefully and then passed it over to the soldier nearest him, who promptly went over to the olive-green jeep that was parked nearby.

"Any other I.D.?"

I produced my Nova Scotia driver's license, my Social Insurance Card, and, once again, my Nova Scotia Teacher's Union card. While he was checking these out I noticed that the soldier in the jeep was typing away at a lap-top computer, having raised a very large antenna on the back of the jeep.

The others returned my documents, and the three of us stood there in silence, staring at the soldier in the jeep. For

Royal Yacht, Kintyre Peninsula, Scotland.

the next five minutes nobody moved, and nothing was said. With each moment growing more uncomfortable than the last, the soldier in the jeep closed up his computer and walked over to my car.

"Were you ever in Northern Ireland?"

At the mention of this the other two became very, very, serious.

"Yes," I replied.

"In July, 1983?"

"Yes, but…how do you know that?"

"Were you and your mate travelling by motorbike?"

"Yes."

"On holiday?"

"Yes."

There was a long pause, and, with a broad smile, he returned my passport.

"He's O.K. Canadian school teacher on holiday. He and his mate were stopped ten years ago just outside Belfast. Travel documents not in order. No Green Cards."

I was relieved when the other two relaxed and shouldered their weapons. Now it was my turn to ask some questions.

Yes, it was indeed the Royal Yacht Britannia. The Royal Family spends the month of August each year at their summer residence in Balmoral Castle, near the village of Pitlochry in the Grampian mountains. The Royal Yacht usually spends the month of August cruising in the Hebrides, since most members of the Royal Family enjoy the peace and serenity of the islands, as well as the chance to relax away from the prying eyes of the world's press.

"Not Diana though," one of them offered. "She hated it up here. Too cold. Too wet. Too boring!"

Secluded beach party setting for the Royal Party,
Kintyre Peninsula, Scotland.

The heavy security was necessary because there was 'A Royal Person' aboard the Britannia.

"Not now though," the fellow continued. "See that launch! It's bringing a 'Royal' ashore to that little beach you see over there. It's one of their favourite picnic sites."

They would not tell me who this 'Royal Person' was. I was, however, allowed to take pictures of the Royal Yacht, the Royal Launch, and the beach area—everything but the soldiers.

"Tell me, just where did you get through to on that little computer, and how did you know about Ireland?" I finally asked.

"I bounced off a bloody satellite and verified your passport with Canada. That checked out. Then I went into our main computer in London and found a file concerning your meeting with the Cheshire regiment in Northern Ireland. You're a travelling man, mate!"

We shook hands and they followed me back to my car.

"One last question!" I asked.

"Sure."

"Is that a warship in the background?"

"Yes. A battle cruiser, to be exact. Just to make sure that no vessel comes too close to the Britannia. After all, Northern Ireland is only forty miles away!"

With that, they waved me through the checkpoint.

Celtic Education

MY GREAT-GRANDFATHER, Hughie Gillis, came to Nova Scotia from Scotland in 1821. He was all of three years old when the immigrant ship carrying him and the rest of his family arrived in Pictou. Two years later the family moved to Inverness County on Cape Breton Island, because the good land in the northern portion of mainland Nova Scotia had already been taken.

Although Hughie was too young to have any recollection of Scotland, his father Angus would undoubtedly have had vivid memories of the land around Loch Morar. After two Canadian winters, he would also have had fond memories of the gentler winters that the warm waters of the Gulf Stream bring to mainland Scotland and the Hebrides.

Angus would have smiled, however, as his vessel made the crossing from Pictou County to Inverness County, on the western side of Cape Breton. Standing on deck, he would have watched with great interest as the low lying land around Pictou gradually gave way to the uplands of Cape St. George, in Antigonish County.

I am sure he would have been positively beaming once the heavily forested outline of the Mabou Highlands came into view. This was more like it. A man born and raised in the Scottish Highlands would more than likely have preferred to spend the rest of his days in a similar landscape.

Memorial cairn to Malcolm Gillis, the 'Margaree Bard.' Upper Margaree, Inverness County, Cape Breton, Nova Scotia.

After landing in Port Hood, and spending a little time with fellow immigrants in the Judique-Creignish area, he made his way to the valley of the Upper Margaree River. There, on the top of a beautiful little mountain less than two miles from Lake Ainslie, he set down permanent roots in the New World.

Even at this early date, the best shore land in Inverness County would already have been claimed by preceding Scottish immigrants. As the land along the coast filled up, the next round of settlers were forced to move inland, following the gentle contours of the fertile river valleys. The really lucky ones wound up on fertile land around the shores of Lake Ainslie. Angus, however, was just a little too late.

But I don't think he was too concerned. Once the trees were cleared from his new mountain, the view in front of him was splendid. He could look to the west, across the newly cleared meadows along the river, and see the hills of Kiltarlity on the other side.

We have no way of knowing whether his ancestral home in Scotland had been on the shores of Loch Morar or back in the hills. In either case, his location less than two miles from the shores of Lake Ainslie must have provided him with an additional comfort.

The third wave of settlers did not fare quite so well. Now that the choice land along the coast and the river valleys had been taken, the only option left was to literally head

Panoramic view from abandoned farmhouse
(still standing), MacKinnon Brook, Mabou Highlands,
Cape Breton, Nova Scotia.

for the hills, or the back lands. The land here was unusually poor, stubborn to clear, and difficult to farm.

Over a period of time and with great effort, the first two waves of settlers developed prosperous farms and a relatively high standard of living. They and their descendants were certainly much better off than they had been in Scotland.

The third wave, those who moved to the back lands or 'the rear' as it was often called, often found that their situation had not, in fact, improved. They had crossed the ocean, only to find themselves second-class settlers, on second-class land!

The farms along the coast and in the river valleys usually became self-sufficient within a generation. They often grew more crops than they needed for themselves and thus had a surplus that could be sold for a profit. The same held true for sheep and cattle.

This was not the case in the rear, however. For most, it was an unrelenting struggle just to survive. What crops they could grow were often of poor quality, and the absence of suitable pastures for their animals was a serious disadvantage.

In order to make ends meet, men from the rear would usually hire themselves out as seasonal labourers to the owners of the more affluent farms in the valleys or along the shore. Others would find seasonal work in fishing and lumbering and return to the rear for the winter months.

By the middle of this century, however, there were very few families left in the rear, whether in Cape Breton, or in mainland Nova Scotia. In Cape Breton, for example, The Mabou Highlands had been deserted, as well as the

View from Broad Cove Chapel, Inverness County, with panoramic view of entire Mabou Highlands (twenty miles wide) in the background. Cape Breton, Nova Scotia.

rear of Boisdale and the rear of Beaver Cove.

Even so, if you know where to look, you can still find traces of the families who lived in the rear.

Stone foundations, abandoned wells, and farm boundaries marked off by crude fences built of stone signify that you have found the remains of someone's home. It is especially telling to see the hand-hewn timbers that are held together with wooden pegs, because they signify that the homesteader could not afford iron nails!

A newcomer arriving in the hills of Upper Margaree, in the early part of the nineteenth century would have seen that the lay of the land, in the valleys of the Margaree River, is quite similar to the lay of the land around Loch Morar. The big difference, of course, is the absence of any natural forest in that part of Scotland. Angus must have been quite shocked when he and his fellow immigrants first sighted the primeval forest that blankets Cape Breton and mainland Nova Scotia.

Since the immigrant ships did not leave Scotland until late spring or early summer, it would have been a difficult task for the new settlers to clear land and plant a crop. More than likely, when they arrived in Pictou they probably spent the first winter as guests of other settlers who had arrived before.

(Archival records indicate that the original Scottish settlers in Nova Scotia would probably not have survived their first winter had it not been for the help and friendship of the Micmac. After all, who could be better to teach these newcomers the tricks of survival in a new and potentially hostile land, than the original inhabitants! The nature of the relationship between the aboriginal inhabitants and the various newcomers is an area that calls out for a great deal of research.)

The same would have happened when Angus moved to Cape Breton. It is likely that he made one or more trips to Cape Breton, however, before actually moving his family there. With the help of friends, he may even have cleared some of the land the year before his family moved.

We do know, however, that Cape Breton at the beginning of the nineteenth century was very thinly settled and quite underdeveloped from an economic point of view. Less than three thousand non-native people were living on the island.

A few were Scots from mainland Nova Scotia or Prince Edward Island. Others were Loyalists, who had come to Cape Breton after the end of the American Revolutionary War in 1776. There were also a small number of Irish, who had crossed the Cabot Strait from Newfoundland.

The vast majority, however, were French-speaking Acadians who had settled in several areas around the coast. They mostly fished cod, which at that time was the mainstay of the local economy. The interior of the island was basically untouched, with virgin forest stretching down to the shores of the Bras D'Or Lakes. Only the native Micmac inhabited the interior.

By 1805, the first substantial influx of Scottish settlers had begun, most of whom came from either the Highlands or the Hebrides. By 1850, more than twenty thousand oth-

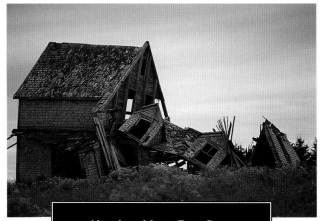

Abandoned farm, River Denys Mountain, Inverness County, Cape Breton, Nova Scotia.

ers had followed, and people of Scottish descent outnumbered all of the others by a ratio of two to one.

At mid-century, the population of Cape Breton Island was in excess of fifty thousand. By this time, the best land had been spoken for, so that any new immigrants from Scotland usually continued directly to Upper Canada or the United States. As the forests were cleared, agriculture gradually replaced fishing as the island's primary economic resource. Lumbering and shipbuilding were also starting to come into their own.

It was into this transplanted Celtic society, only one generation removed from Scotland, that my grandfather Malcolm was born in 1856. At the time of his death in 1929, he was known to Celtic Cape Breton as 'The Margaree Bard,' having achieved a certain renown as a Gaelic poet, and songwriter. His renown was even greater in the Old Country, largely because a book of his Gaelic poetry and songs was published in Glasgow in the 1930s.

A school teacher and the father of eighteen children, he even taught for a year in the French-speaking village of Cheticamp. It appears that he had more than a working knowledge of the French language!

Grandfather was very well educated—cultured even— but he was by no means unique. In the latter part of the nineteenth century, the Celtic sections of Cape Breton and mainland Nova Scotia produced a steady stream of highly educated and very talented young men.

The talent part was easy. You were either born with it, or you were not.

It was the education part of this puzzle, however, that posed an enigma. How, in the rural areas of Cape Breton

The Lone Sheiling, Pleasant Bay, Victoria County,
Cape Breton, Nova Scotia.

and mainland Nova Scotia, did people acquire a sophisticated level of education, an education that was often soundly grounded in the European Classics?

Dougald MacFarlane, a first cousin and retired university professor from Halifax, came up with the answer. He found it in Upper Margaree of all places, on our ancestral hill.

Dougald has the distinct advantage of being fluent in Gaelic, an attribute that is of immense value when attempting to get precise information from older Celtic people.

He started with Aunt Mary, age ninety-two. Born in Port Hood, and christened Mary Gillis, she went to the Nova Scotia Teacher's College in Truro back in the days when it was known as the 'Normal College.'

She taught school in Port Hood for a few years and then moved to 'The Boston States' in the early 1920s. Aunt Mary worked in Boston as a domestic (maid), at a salary that was more than double what she had made as a teacher in Cape Breton.

While at a 'down-east' square dance she met my Uncle Jack, the second oldest of the Bard's eighteen children. He was working as a carpenter in Boston at the time, and happened to be playing the fiddle with 'The Inverness Serenaders,' a Celtic band that had been assembled by his brother Alex.

They married in 1931, after Jack returned from Boston to take over the family farm following the death of his father in 1929.

Aunt Mary told Dougald about the itinerant teachers who travelled throughout the rural areas of Inverness County in the middle and latter part of the last century. Some were school teachers, while others were highly qualified musicians, many with advanced training. One such person was Malcolm MacLellan, also known as 'Malcolm the Scholar.'

Malcolm and his younger brother, John, were born in Scotland, the children of a poor crofter. The landlord, an educated and wealthy man, recognized the latent intelligence in the two young boys and took it upon himself to provide them with an education.

They were first given a thorough schooling in Gaelic and English and then they were sent to Europe for a few years to put the finishing touches on their education. While on the Continent they studied the Classics, and acquired a working knowledge of Latin and French.

After returning from Europe, they made their way to Nova Scotia. John went on to teach at the original campus of St. Francis Xavier University in Arichat, while Malcolm became an itinerant teacher in western Cape Breton and north eastern Nova Scotia.

When the young university moved to the village of Antigonish in the early 1850s, John continued to teach in Cape Breton. Working as an itinerant teacher, like his brother, he gave eager students such as my grandfather a solid grounding in Gaelic, Latin, English, and French.

I think it is safe to assume that my grandfather and his peers came by their formal musical education in the same

The first motor car seen in Boisdale, Cape Breton, at the wedding of my maternal grandparents, 1914. Hector MacLean (groom) behind the wheel, with his new bride Catherine (Nicholson) beside him. Hector lived to the age of eighty-three, but never learned to drive!

manner, from itinerant teachers who had been educated in Scotland and, in some cases, on the Continent.

While Dougald was visiting at my home, in early February of 1994, I was able to introduce him to Marianne Cloitre, a young exchange student from Brittany in France. A woman of Celtic descent, Marianne was taking a year of English Immersion at Memorial High School in Sydney Mines.

In the course of our conversation Marianne mentioned that she had graduated from high school in France with thirty-two credits—an amazing number in only three years.

Her school day started at eight o'clock, ended at five o'clock, and she had one hour for lunch. So she therefore put in a full day, the same as any working person. Among her studies were four languages; French, English, German, and Greek!

(In Nova Scotia, only seventeen credits are required to graduate from high school, and there are no language requirements, other than English.)

As a professional educator, I found it rather embarrassing to explain to Marianne that my grandfather in rural Cape Breton probably received a better basic education in the nineteenth century, than do most of the students in Nova Scotia in the closing years of the twentieth!

Celtic Music

I FIRST MET DONALD RIDDELL late one warm summer evening in 1979, when I went to pick him up at the airport in Sydney. The director of a Celtic Chamber Orchestra from Inverness, Scotland, Donald and sixteen other young violinists had just flown in from the Old Country.

Donald, his wife Jill, and two young musicians, were billeted at my home in North Sydney. His young orchestra, with Donald directing and playing the fiddle, were to appear as special guests at the Antigonish Highland Games. Following this they would tour for two weeks, appearing at numerous Celtic gatherings in Nova Scotia and Prince Edward Island.

The next morning, the residents of Upper Archibald Avenue (myself included) were startled by the skirling of the great Highland bagpipe. Donald, up for an early morning walk, had come upon a neighbour, Brenda Ryan, who was sitting outside trying to fix the reed on her chanter. (The chanter is the part of the pipes that is held in the hands, for fingering the notes.)

After fixing the problem without too much difficulty, he then offered to try the pipes to see if they were in tune. What Brenda and her neighbours did not know, however, was that Pipe Major Donald Riddell was one of the finest pipers in all of Scotland.

He had won many awards for his piping, not only in Scotland, but in England as well. As a young Territorial Army piper in the Queen's Own Cameron Highlanders,

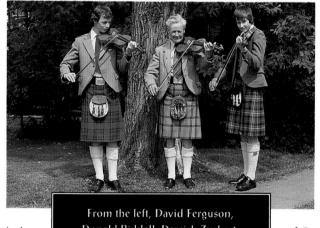

From the left, David Ferguson, Donald Riddell, Derrick Zuckert.

he was chosen to play at the funeral of King George V in 1936. Considering it a singular honour, he wrote a special tune for the occasion. The "Lament For The Death Of King George V" was later recorded and widely distributed throughout Britain.

When World War Two broke out he joined the Lord Lovat Scouts, as Pipe Major. Donald quickly built their regimental band into one of the finest units of its kind in the British Army. With the Lovat Scouts he saw combat in Italy and Greece, for Donald was a highly trained commando as well as a musician. In the closing years of the war he spent time in western Canada, where he helped train Canadian commandos.

Once he had the pipes fired up, there was no stopping him. Dressed in his kilt and full Scottish regalia he proceeded to march up and down the sidewalk in front of Brenda's home, as incredulous neighbours rushed outside to see just what was going on.

At one point he paused, eyes tightly shut, as he reverently fingered the notes of the lament he had played on the occasion of that Royal funeral, many years ago. Then he was off again with a selection of strathspeys, followed by a number of reels. The music reverberated off the walls of the neighbourhood homes and filled the air with the sounds of Scotland.

His military background was unknown to me at that time, as it was to most outside of his own family. A modest

Donald Riddell (left) instructs his grandson, Colin Spankie
on the violin. South Clunes, Loch Ness, Scotland.

man, he refused to be drawn into conversation regarding his military background. He much preferred to speak about music.

Two years later I would stay for a week at his home in the mountains overlooking Loch Ness. Each day I would go out touring on my motorcycle, and return in the evening for whisky and wonderful conversation, most of it about music.

Donald was the first to make me aware of the special correlation between the traditional music of Scotland and the traditional music of Cape Breton. I must admit that prior to his visit to Nova Scotia I had not really given the matter much thought.

As anyone of Celtic descent, who grew up in a musical home in Cape Breton, can attest, the term 'Celtic' was seldom, if ever, used. Your parents referred to themselves as being of Scotch or Irish descent. The music that my father and mother played was Scottish music, while the music that Johnny Wilmot played was Irish.

That was not to say that Johnny didn't play Scotch fiddle tunes, and my mother didn't play Irish piano music. They did. It was just that the term 'Celtic' was not in vogue, unless you were an academic.

It was Donald who pointed out that the Cape Breton style of traditional fiddle music, which had come over during the Highland Clearances, had virtually disappeared in Scotland. And this is what I discovered when I made my first visit.

Over the last 250 years, fiddle music in Scotland had gone in two separate directions: classical and folk. (Classical

Young stepdancers, Mabou Ceilidh, Mabou, Nova Scotia.

in this sense refers to formal instruction by a professional musician or educator. Folk refers to a musician who is largely self-taught.)

The classical tradition was centered in the large urban areas of Lowland Scotland, while the folk tradition was most intense in the rural areas of the Highlands and Islands.

By 1775, Edinburgh had a reputation as a classical music center that was the equal of any in Europe. For a while it even surpassed the centers of musical life in England. It had a music school that employed talented instructors who had been brought over from the Continent, as well as several top instrumentalists and vocalists.

The folk scene was somewhat different, and was to undergo a dramatic transformation in the period after Bonnie Prince Charlie and the Rebellion of 1745. The

restrictions that were imposed on the population of the Highlands and Islands extended to music. The bagpipes were banned, the fiddle was frowned upon, and the Gaelic folk song tradition was severely curtailed, as was the language itself.

Over the next one hundred years, the authentic folk traditions were restricted to an increasingly smaller area in the Highlands and the Islands. By the middle of the twentieth century, they had mostly disappeared.

The vast majority of the Scots who immigrated to Atlantic Canada came from the Highlands and the Hebrides during this same period of time, and they brought their traditional music styles with them. but this leaves us with an intriguing question. Since these immigrants settled in all parts of the Maritimes, why is the truly traditional fiddle style found only in Cape Breton?

The answer, of course, has to do with assimilation. The process by which immigrants are absorbed into society, and gradually lose most of their customs and traditions, was a very real fact of life for all newcomers. Although most made an attempt to hold on to the old ways, for many it was a losing cause.

By the middle of this century, the traditional fiddle music of the immigrant Scot, as well as his language, was found in only a few isolated locations. Places such as the Codroy valley in western Newfoundland, and parts of Antigonish and Guysborough counties on mainland Nova Scotia, made a valiant effort to preserve the past. There were still Highland Games, square dances, and the isolated milling frolic.

Rural Cape Breton was different, mainly because it was a bit more isolated from the rapidly changing world of the mid-twentieth century. The old language held on longer too. Tucked away in the hills and glens of Inverness, Richmond, and Victoria counties, the older folk still said their prayers in Gaelic and continued to sing the traditional songs in their native tongue.

Many saw the advent of television as the final blow. How could Gaelic and traditional fiddle music survive in the face of this modern telecommunications marvel, which

Waiting to perform, Mabou Ceilidh, Mabou, Nova Scotia.

suddenly provided instant access to a full range of music from across North America?

In the winter of 1971, a strange thing then happened. A CBC television documentary appeared with the intriguing name: 'The Vanishing Cape Breton Fiddler.' Its thesis was simple and to the point. The Gaelic language would soon disappear as the last of the old folks passed away, and so too would their traditional fiddle music. It said the demise of Gaelic and Cape Breton style fiddle music was rapidly approaching.

The program hit a raw nerve with many in Cape Breton, a Celtic raw nerve. Something quite spontaneous and most unusual took place. Within a year the Cape Breton Fiddler's Association sprang to life, a gathering of like–minded individuals whose sole intent was to disprove the central premise of the television documentary. And they succeeded beyond their wildest dreams!

In July, 1973, over ten thousand people showed up in a field behind the Catholic church in Glendale, Inverness County. Tourists passing by on the Trans-Canada Highway must have thought that a major rock festival was under way.

Although few appreciated it at the time, what was under way was a major reaffirmation of the central role of traditional fiddle music in the lives of Nova Scotians. The people who came that day represented a cross-section of the island, and of many parts of mainland Nova Scotia. A significant number had also come from the New England states. Many in attendance were neither Scotch nor Irish.

What everyone shared in common was a love for traditional fiddle music, and there were more than 130 traditional fiddlers to entertain them. The music started early in the afternoon and went on well into the night. Few, if any, left.

There were few solos, since the number of waiting participants was just too high. There were fiddle duets, trios, and quartets. Step dancers and Gaelic singers took the music into still another dimension.

Three young Barra MacNeils, perform on stage at the Highland Village in Iona, Cape Breton, Nova Scotia, in 1974. Kyle (fiddle); Sheamus (piano); Stewart (step dancing); and Donald MacLean (step dancer).

When they all got up on stage together for the grand finale, I remember thinking to myself: "This is a larger string section than the Boston Symphony, or any other orchestra for that matter!"

And so it turned out that the invention that would supposedly sound the death knell for traditional fiddle music in Cape Breton, brought about its revival.

Fast forward to 1994. We no longer refer to Scottish music or Irish music in Cape Breton; it is all Celtic music.

Celtic music is no longer found in only a few small rural locations, and listened to by an aging, and rapidly diminishing, population.

It can now be heard on national radio and television, and its star performers are rapidly becoming house-

hold names right across the country.

The Celtic music of Cape Breton has not only gone national, it has gone international.

Rita MacNeil of Big Pond, Cape Breton County, was the first to develop a significant following outside her own region. Although not a Celtic artist in the 'technical' sense of the term, she has written songs that draw quite heavily on her Celtic past, and she has eloquently communicated the hopes and aspirations of her generation of Cape Bretoners.

Cape Breton's premier musical groups, The Rankin Family from Mabou and The Barra MacNeils from Sydney Mines, are 'pure' Celtic in the best sense of the word. These immensely gifted siblings have recently signed lucrative recording contracts with international record companies. In 1994, The Rankin Family walked away with four Juno awards: Best Canadian entertainer and best group of the year, best country group and best single.

A whole new galaxy of young, extremely polished, Celtic musicians has appeared on the scene.

Natalie MacMaster, age twenty-one, won the award for 'Instrumental Artist of the Year' at the East Coast Music Awards in 1994. Then the native of Troy, Inverness County, promptly flew off for engagements in Florida, Washington, D.C., and Auckland, New Zealand.

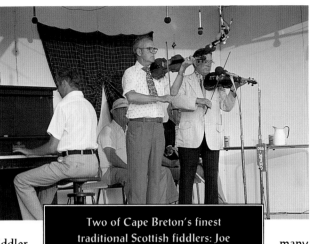

Ashley MacIssac, age eighteen, played with the internationally renowned Irish traditional group 'The Chieftains' on a cross-Canada tour in the fall of 1993. They then promptly invited him to appear with them on stage, at Carnegie Hall in New York, for their traditional St. Patrick's Day Concert in March, 1994. The left-handed fiddler from Cregnish, Inverness County, has also recorded two tracks for a new album by Edie Brickell, the wife of well known singer-songwriter Paul Simon.

Two of Cape Breton's finest traditional Scottish fiddlers: Joe MacLean (left) and Bill Lamey. Glendale Fiddle Concert, Inverness County, Cape Breton, Nova Scotia.

What would Donald Riddell make of all this? Or my grandfather Malcolm Gillis, the Margaree Bard?

What is going on, of course, is the North American revival of an interest in all things Celtic, led in this case by a contingent of young and talented musicians from Cape Breton Island.

Celtic music is certainly not new. It has always, in one form or another, been a vital part of the rural social scene here in Cape Breton.

What is fascinating, however, is the fact that many individuals who had lost contact with their Celtic roots, through no fault of their own, are now discovering a musical window that opens onto a long–forgotten world. Equally amazing is the wave of widespread appreciation for the music of Natalie McMaster and her peers, who are breathing new life into an ancient tradition whose time has clearly come.

Rannie Recommends

Guidance for Visitors in the Celtic World

Cape Breton

1. **The Cabot Trail.** The most spectacular drive in eastern North America. A 184 mile route that winds its way from the shores of St. Ann's bay (Scottish/Celtic) to the shores of the Gulf of St. Lawrence (French/Celtic).

2. **Money Point.** The most northerly point in Nova Scotia. Over 200 shipwrecks are known to have occurred in the waters around this rocky headland. Early settlers claimed that they could find gold and silver coins on the shores, after severe fall and winter storms.

3. **Meat Cove.** The end of the (dirt) road in northern Cape Breton. Spectacular scenery, with rugged cliffs that drop precipitously to the ocean. The road is not for the faint of heart.

4. **The High Capes.** A series of 800 foot cliffs, located on the north western tip of the Cape Breton Highlands. These is no access by road. Hikers face a tough slog, over boggy and mountainous terrain.

5. **The Mabou Highlands.** A lovely set of mountains, with community pastures on the extensive upland plateau. There are overgrown roads, abandoned farms, and numerous hiking routes that skirt the sea.

6. **Mabou Coal Mines.** A scenic gem, hidden away between the Highlands and the sea. At the turn of the century, undersea coal was mined in this area.

7. **River Denys Mountains.** Abandoned farms, logged-out plateaus, and a hidden waterfall. The oldest wooden church on the island stands on the summit. Religious services are held twice a year.

8. **Marble Mountain.** One of the island's best kept secrets. Spectacular location on the shores of the Bras D'Or Lakes. At the turn of the century, a quarry shipped high–quality marble to Halifax, Boston, and New York.

9. **Little Anse.** The end of the road in Isle Madame. In the minds of many, the most picturesque and colourful harbour on the Atlantic seaboard. A hiking trail leads to Cap Rouge, and a view of one of the few remaining manned lighthouses in Nova Scotia.

10. **Highland Village**, Hector's Point, Iona. A splendid reconstruction of the lifestyle of the early Celtic inhabitants of the island. Superb panoramic views take in all four counties of Cape Breton.

Ireland

These are my personal suggestions for the 'Top 10' Celtic attractions in Ireland. They are not listed in any particular order of merit.

1. **Skellig Michael**, County Kerry. One of the Celtic world's truly unique places. A 'must-see' for anyone with an interest in early Celtic Christianity.

2. **Dun Aengus**, County Galway. A truly awe-inspiring stone fortification, situated on the edge of the Celtic world.

3. **The Aran Islands**, County Galway. Three islands, six miles off the west coast, that appear in early Celtic artifacts. Their inhabitants have long been thought of as living examples of the ancient Celtic culture.

4. **The cliffs at Slieve League**, County Donegal. At 1,972 feet, these are the highest marine cliffs in Europe or the British Isles. Early monastic ruins on the top.

5. **Carrantuohill**, County Kerry. At 3,414 feet, it is the highest mountain in Ireland. Views from the summit encompass the sea, lakes, and hills of the County Kerry.

6. **The Dingle Peninsula**, County Kerry. Superb mountains and coastal scenery as well as an extraordinary number of prehistoric and early Christian remains.

7. **Newgrange.** The largest and most impressive of three burial mounds that predate the Egyptian Pyramids. Numerous other burial mounds, standing stones, and prehistoric ruins, are found in the vicinity.

8. **The Burren**, County of Clare. Fifty square miles of weathered and eroded limestone. This great upland wilderness, on the edge of Galway Bay, contains numerous prehistoric remains such as stone forts and burial mounds.

9. **Carrowkeel Passage Graves**, County of Sligo. A total of 16 megalithic passage graves are situated on a series of peaks in the Bricklieve Mountains.

10. **Glendalough**, County of Wicklow. Site of a famous sixth century monastery, located in one of the most beautiful glens in Ireland. Numerous religious and secular archaeological remains are found in the vicinity.

Scotland

These are my personal suggestions for the 'Top 10' Celtic attractions in Scotland. They are not listed in any particular order of merit.

1. **The main ridge of the Cuillin Mountains**, Isle of Skye, from the village of Elgol. According to the Scottish Mountaineering Guide, this view is "the most incredible panorama of mountains and sea in the world."

2. **Loch Coruisk, Isle of Skye.** The most imposing combination of loch and mountain scenery in all of Scotland.

3. **The 'Vitrified' Iron-Age fort from the top of 'An Sgurr,'** Isle of Eigg. One of the great Celtic mysteries, and a scenic viewpoint 'par excellence'!

4. **The Norse–influenced Isle of Rhum.** This mysterious 'Forbidden Isle' is owned by the Nature Conservancy.

5. **The trek from 'Barnhill' to the cliffs overlooking the Gulf of Corrievrecken**, Isle of Jura, Inner Hebrides. Splendid scenery of mountain and moor, with a view of the second largest whirlpool in the world, weather permitting.

6. **Fingal's Cave**, Isle of Staffa.

7. **The east–coast road**, Isle of Harris, Outer Hebrides. A treacherous little one–land track, with severe hairpin turns and many blind bends. Not for the faint of heart, or for large vehicles of any kind. Post-glacial scenery that is absolutely mind-boggling.

8. **'Bealach nam Bo'** (Pass of the Cattle), Applecross, West Highlands. This spectacular pass zigzags from sea level to 2,054 feet, as it climbs to the summit of the Applecross Mountains. The ascent is thrilling, if you don't look back; the descent will test your nerve, and your brakes!

9. **The Cape Wrath Lighthouse** is situated 300 feet above the ocean, on the extreme north western tip of the Scottish mainland. This marked the point where the Viking longships turned south for the Hebrides and the west coast of the British Isles.

10. **Glencoe**, West Highlands. The most scenic and most infamous glen in Scotland, scene of the Massacre of Glencoe. In February, 1692, a group of Campbells murdered forty members of the Clan MacDonald in their sleep. The Campbells had been taken in and given food and shelter for a period of twelve days, before turning on their hosts.

Fingal's Cave, Isle of Staffa.